# Chemistry NOW!
## 11–14

## Teacher's Resource Book

# Chemistry NOW! 11–14
# Teacher's Resource Book

Peter D Riley

**JOHN MURRAY**

**Titles in this series:**
*Biology Now! 11–14* Pupil's Book    ISBN 0 7195 7548 6
*Chemistry Now! 11–14* Pupil's Book    ISBN 0 7195 7546 X
*Physics Now! 11–14* Pupil's Book    ISBN 0 7195 7544 3

*Biology Now! 11–14* Teacher's Resource Book    ISBN 0 7195 7549 4
*Chemistry Now! 11–14* Teacher's Resource Book    ISBN 0 7195 7547 8
*Physics Now! 11–14* Teacher's Resource Book    ISBN 0 7195 7545 1

**Acknowledgements**

I am most grateful to Kerry Mitchell for providing the practical activities for Chapters 5, 6, 9, 13 and 14. Also, thanks to Peter Borrows (CLEAPSS) for providing safety advice on activities and procedures throughout the text, and to Jeffery Holdsworth for advising on the application of information technology to this book.

The Key Stage 3 test and mark scheme (pages 93–110) have been reproduced from *Key Stage 3 science tests, Tier 5–7, Paper 1, 2, Level 8, extensions and mark scheme, SCAA 1997* with the kind permission of the Qualifications and Curriculum Authority.

Material from the National Curriculum on pages 111–114 is Crown Copyright and is reproduced by permission of the controller of HMSO.

**Photo credits**

With thanks to Professor Mackenzie for kindly providing the photos for use on page 100.

© Peter D Riley 1999

First published in 1999
by John Murray (Publishers) Ltd
50 Albemarle Street
London W1S 4BD

Reprinted 2000

All rights reserved. The material in this publication is copyright but permission is given to teachers to make copies of the Investigation sheets, Worksheets, 13+ Question bank and Key Stage 3 test for one-time use as instructional material within their own school (or other educational institution). This permission does not extend to the making of copies for use outside the institution in which they are made (e.g. in a resource centre), and the material may not be copied in unlimited quantities, kept on behalf of others, passed on or sold to third parties or stored for future use in a retrieval system. If you wish to use the material in any way other than as specified you must apply in writing to the publishers.

Layouts by Ann Samuel
Illustrations by Barking Dog Art
Cover design by John Townson/Creation

Typeset in Garamond Light by Wearset, Boldon,
Tyne and Wear
Printed and bound by Selwood Printing Ltd. West Sussex

A catalogue entry for this title is available from the British Library

ISBN 0 7195 7547 8

# Contents

| | | |
|---|---|---|
| | **Introduction** | **vii** |
| | Investigation sheet 1 | xi |
| | Investigation sheet 2 | xii |
| | Investigation sheet 3 | xiii |
| **Chapter 1** | **Introducing chemistry** | **1** |
| | Answers | 1 |
| | IT input | 3 |
| | Activities | 3 |
| | Worksheets | 5 |
| **Chapter 2** | **The world of matter** | **8** |
| | Answers | 8 |
| | IT input | 10 |
| | Activities | 10 |
| | Worksheet | 14 |
| **Chapter 3** | **Separation of mixtures** | **15** |
| | Answers | 15 |
| | IT input | 16 |
| | Activities | 16 |
| | Worksheets | 21 |
| **Chapter 4** | **Elements and atoms** | **23** |
| | Answers | 23 |
| | IT input | 24 |
| | Activities | 24 |
| | Worksheets | 25 |
| **Chapter 5** | **Chemical reactions** | **27** |
| | Answers | 27 |
| | IT input | 28 |
| | Activities | 28 |
| | Worksheets | 31 |
| **Chapter 6** | **Acids and bases** | **37** |
| | Answers | 37 |
| | IT input | 38 |
| | Activities | 38 |
| | Worksheets | 40 |
| **Chapter 7** | **Air** | **47** |
| | Answers | 47 |
| | IT input | 48 |
| | Activities | 48 |
| | Worksheets | 50 |

# CONTENTS

| | | | |
|---|---|---|---|
| **Chapter 8** | **The Earth – a rocky planet** | | **52** |
| | Answers | | 52 |
| | IT input | | 54 |
| | Activities | | 54 |
| | Worksheet | | 56 |
| **Chapter 9** | **Metals and non-metals** | | **57** |
| | Answers | | 57 |
| | IT input | | 59 |
| | Activities | | 59 |
| | Worksheets | | 62 |
| **Chapter 10** | **Earth materials** | | **67** |
| | Answers | | 67 |
| | IT input | | 70 |
| | Activities | | 70 |
| | Worksheets | | 72 |
| **Chapter 11** | **The chemical industry** | | **74** |
| | Answers | | 74 |
| | IT input | | 75 |
| | Activities | | 76 |
| | Worksheet | | 77 |
| **Chapter 12** | **Chemicals and the environment** | | **78** |
| | Answers | | 78 |
| | IT input | | 80 |
| | Activities | | 80 |
| | Worksheet | | 82 |
| **Chapter 13** | **The periodic table** | | **83** |
| | Answers | | 83 |
| | IT input | | 84 |
| | Activities | | 84 |
| | Worksheets | | 85 |
| **Chapter 14** | **Using formulae** | | **87** |
| | Answers | | 87 |
| | IT input | | 87 |
| | Activities | | 87 |
| | Worksheets | | 88 |
| | **13+ Question bank** | | **90** |
| | Answers to the 13+ Question bank | | 92 |
| | **Key Stage 3 test** | | **93** |
| | Key Stage 3 test mark scheme | | 103 |
| | **Meeting the demands of the National Curriculum or Common Entrance Examination at 13+** | | **111** |

# Introduction

The content of the *Chemistry Now! 11–14* Pupil's Book is supported by the activities in this book to provide a course which consolidates the work of Key Stage 2 and builds a foundation for work at Key Stage 4 and beyond. It is hoped that the material in these books will stimulate more pupils to consider a career in science by appreciating their scientific heritage and enjoying science as a valuable human activity. A second aim is to develop the scientific literacy of all pupils so that they are equipped to assess, evaluate and make decisions on issues with a scientific element in their future lives, both at a personal level and at a level which affects their community and the world environment.

## About the Pupil's Book

This book is aimed at the more able pupil. The text is divided into two parts – the main text and boxed sections. The main text aims to provide content for the Common Entrance Examination at 13+ and for Key Stage 3 tests. The objective of the boxed sections is to present science as a human activity. Both the main text and the boxed sections have questions which test a range of skills.

## Questions

The questions have been selected to test a range of intellectual competencies as set out in Bloom's taxonomy. The following is a very brief account of these competencies and how they are related to each other. It is only intended as a very simple introduction but it is hoped that the information given here may help in the assessment of the pupils' answers and in the construction of any supplementary questions you may like to add to those in the Pupil's Book and to the activities offered here.

The competencies are:

1 **Knowledge**. There is a range of kinds of knowledge, including a knowledge of facts, terms, criteria, classification, trends, methods, principles and theories.
2 **Comprehension**. This deals with the translation of one form of information into another, such as illustrating a general principle or expressing raw data in tables and graphs. Comprehension also deals with the interpretation of material and the ability to draw conclusions, make predictions and identify any factors which may limit the accuracy of a prediction.
3 **Application**. To demonstrate application, the pupil must remember a range of facts and principles and select those that are appropriate to the task.
4 **Analysis**. This involves the breaking down of the material into parts, the relationships between them and the way that they are organised. It may involve separating facts from hypotheses or identifying the point of view of a writer on a scientific issue.
5 **Synthesis**. This is the re-combining of the parts of analysed material, using previous experience to produce a clear structure or pattern. This may take the form of constructing a hypothesis, devising experimental plans or writing a scientific article or essay.
6 **Evaluation**. This involves the use of criteria to make judgements on ideas, methods and conclusions to experiments, or scientific articles.

Although the competencies may be ranked in a hierarchy from knowledge to evaluation they may also be represented as a cycle, as evaluation leads to new knowledge which in turn leads to new opportunities for comprehension and demonstration of the other competencies:

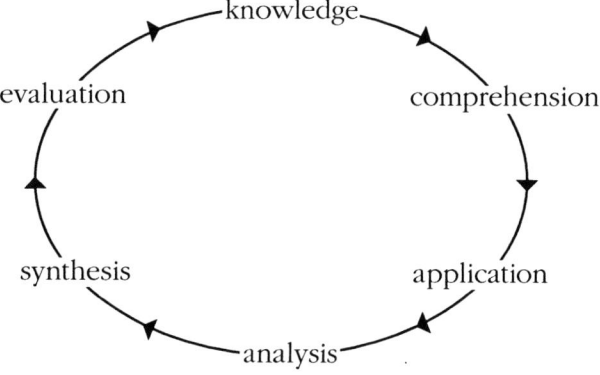

# INTRODUCTION

## Identifying and setting questions to test the range of competencies

The following words may be used in the stem of the question to test the different competencies:

**Knowledge**: when, where, who, name, label, define, identify, show, list.
**Comprehension**: contrast, discuss, interpret, summarise, predict, differentiate, extend.
**Application**: demonstrate, discover, apply, classify.
**Analysis**: compare, separate, explain, arrange, order, divide.
**Synthesis**: plan, formulate, prepare, rewrite, modify, design.
**Evaluation**: assess, rank, judge, conclude.

## For discussion questions

These questions are for small groups of pupils to discuss initially, then the discussion can be broadened to the whole class. The aim is to provide an opportunity to talk about scientific issues, to discover different points of view and to see how a consensus of opinion may develop.

## End of chapter questions

The End of chapter questions are intended to draw together several areas of the chapter. The questions may be used the first time the chapter is completed, or as a starting point when the chapter is re-visited for revision purposes.

## Content of boxed sections

Many of the boxed sections present historical accounts of how scientific ideas developed. It is appreciated that the development of scientific ideas is a very complex topic, with many pieces of research contributing to each idea. To introduce this concept some selection has been made to present simple strands to help the pupils realise:

**a)** how scientists interpret their results according to the terms and theories of their times,
**b)** how scientists use previous work as a starting point or to support their own work,
**c)** that chance plays a part in scientific discovery; and
**d)** that scientists may make important discoveries in some areas of science and yet hold views in other areas which are contrary to current ideas.

By reading the text and answering the questions in these boxed sections it is hoped that the pupils will develop a wider appreciation of scientific investigation and identify some instances in their own investigations that reflect a similar approach.

Some boxed sections deal with everyday applications of the content described in the main text. Many of the questions in these boxes raise issues which the pupils can discuss.

## Answers

Answers to all the questions in the Pupil's Book are given here. In some instances a pupil may wish to display extra knowledge in answering a straightforward question, or the question may encourage the pupil to think more widely. The answers in this book give the simple response to straightforward questions. There may be other responses which can be added to these which take into account the pupils' previous experience. These extra responses may be used to earn the pupils extra credit for their work or to provide additional material which may be used to assess the pupils' attitude, aptitude and general progress.

# About the Teacher's Resource Book

## End of chapter tests

This teacher's book contains a photocopiable End of chapter test for each chapter. The answers to these are given at the end of the answers section for that chapter.

At the end of the book there are two additional sections. One has questions similar to those found in the Common Entrance Examination at 13+ and the other is made up of questions from past Key Stage 3 Science tests. These can be used as preparation for assessment at the end of the course.

## Activities

The activities are described briefly to provide points of focus for practical work to support sections in the Pupil's Book. Each activity is numbered and carries a reference to the section and page it supports in the Pupil's Book, so that the book and activity can be used together.

# INTRODUCTION

Teachers may then build on the suggestions made here. Some activities are supported by a photocopiable worksheet to help in skills assessment and to provide variety in approach.

## Hazard warning symbols

Pupils will need to be familiar with these symbols when undertaking practical experiments in the laboratory.

 Corrosive      Oxidising

 Explosive      Radioactive

 Harmful or irritant      Toxic

 Highly flammable      Eye protection

 Other danger to consider

## Information technology (IT)

The content of the Pupil's Book and the Teacher's Resource Book can be extended by information technology work. As new titles and products are continually entering the market only a few well known ones are mentioned here, but these should provide ideas on how IT work can be applied to the course and how new resources can be incorporated as they become available.

Details of data logging equipment or activities have not been given for this level. Examples from Key Stage 4 courses may be adapted at the teacher's discretion.

## Making graphs

High quality graphing programs exist either on their own or as part of a spreadsheet package, and pupils ought to develop skills of selecting appropriate graph types for the task in hand and develop skills in criticising the software output. The manual graph drawing exercises in the pupil's text and the activities in this book can be replaced with computer generated output as the teacher wishes.

## Using animations

Graphics packages which allow animations to be created quite simply, such as *Animator*, can be used at several points in the Pupil's Book. For example, the pupil's ability to show fractional distillation could be assessed or the teacher could use the program to produce demonstrations.

## Making presentations

There are many software packages for producing presentations. Pupils or teachers could produce slide shows to demonstrate sequences of events. Those that are produced by the pupils can be used to assess their understanding of the work. Most packages have libraries of symbols for chemical hazards and laboratory equipment.

## Using CD-ROMs

CD-ROMs contain a huge volume and variety of information in a very easily accessible form which is motivating at all levels of ability. However, pupils should not be given exercises which allow them uncritically to trawl through the information and print it out without effort, appraisal or understanding – 'virtual homework'. Teachers should refer pupils to CD-ROMs with enthusiasm but also under very tight constraints to ensure that the pupils' output matches the objectives of the exercise. A first exercise could be providing questions to a specific text on a CD-ROM in the style of the questions in the boxed sections of the Pupil's Book. This may help the pupils to realise their task and help them to interact with the material in a more positive way.

The main groups of useful CD-ROMs are:

**Encyclopaedias**, both general and specific, for example *Encarta*, *Grolier*, *Hutchinson's Science Library*, and *Inventors and Inventions*. Chapters 7, 8, 10 and 12 contain material often found in CD-ROMs aimed at Earth Science, Environment Science and Geography. Encyclopaedias usually contain animations, film clips, sounds and photographs as well as text.

**Newspaper and magazine databases**, which may be searched for significant stories and events, such as pollution incidents or new industrial processes.

**Simulations**, which allow pupils to develop their appreciation of complex topics, such as pollution.

# INTRODUCTION

## *Desktop publishing*

Pupils can be given research and publishing work to do, possibly involving CD-ROM, Internet and library investigations with the output produced using a word processor or simple desktop publishing program. Pupils might be asked to produce short biographies or small posters on personalities mentioned in the text in the Pupil's Book. This might lead to a display – the Chemistry Hall of Fame – which can be augmented throughout the course as new personalities are covered in later chapters. The first exercises in this project could be researching a famous scientist, such as Robert Boyle (Chapter 2), Antoine Lavoisier (Chapter 4) or Joseph Priestley (Chapter 9). Lists of scientists to research are shown in the chapter notes in this book, with page references to the Pupil's Book.

## Investigation proformas

The following three photocopiable investigation sheets can be used by the pupils to plan, record, analyse and evaluate their evidence. They can be used with the activities which have the word 'investigate' in their title or with any other investigation you wish to use to assess the pupils' skills in Experimental and Investigative Science (Sc1).

# Investigation sheet 1

■ The idea to be investigated is:

■ The background knowledge I have about this investigation is:

■ I predict that:

■ I believe my prediction to be correct because:

■ The key factors in this investigation are:

■ The key factor I will vary is:

■ The key factors I will control are:

■ I will make the following observations or measurements:

# Investigation sheet 2

■ I will need the following equipment:

■ I will set up and/or carry out my investigation in the following way:

■ I will take the following precautions:

■ I will take these precautions because:

■ I will record my results in this table:

■ The graphs I have produced from these data are attached to this sheet.

# Investigation sheet 3

■ The trends or patterns shown in these results are:


■ The conclusion I draw from my results is that:


■ The background knowledge I am using to support my conclusion is:


■ When I compare my conclusion with my prediction I find that:


■ I believe the evidence is sufficient/not sufficient to support a firm conclusion because:


■ Unusual observations or measurements were due to:


■ If the investigation is to be repeated I suggest the following changes to improve it:

# 1 Introducing chemistry

# Answers

## What is chemistry? (PB page 2)

1 The air gets hot, a flame is produced, smoke is produced, a hissing sound may be made, the amount of wood decreases, the wood changes colour from brown to black, a grey ash is produced.
2 If other people learned about the way they tried to change lead into gold they may have used their ideas and made it for themselves, so the value of the gold would fall.

## Measuring quantities (PB pages 3 and 5)

3 The reading would indicate slightly more liquid in the measuring cylinder than was actually present.
4 19.5°C
5 No – when they take the thermometer bulb out of the liquid the temperature of the air is then being taken and the liquid in the thermometer will expand or contract according to whether the air is warmer or colder than the liquid.
6 Keep the thermometer bulb completely immersed in the liquid until the reading has been taken.

## Bunsen burner (PB page 7)

1 19th Century
2 88
3 Because he used it widely in his work and other scientists began to use it too – he made it popular.
4 It produces a strong, steady heat without smoke.
5 G.R. Kirchhoff, caesium, rubidium
6 49, 50

## Apparatus (PB pages 7 and 8)

7 thermometer, burette, measuring cylinder
8 The tripod and heatproof mat shown in the diagram in the right-hand column may be replaced by an arrow with 'heat' written underneath it.

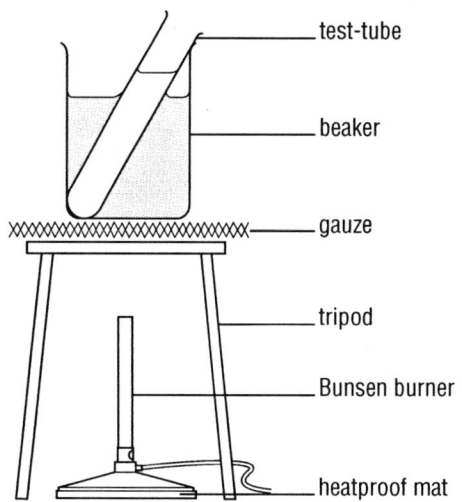

9 30 cm³
10 Read the volume of liquid in the burette, open the tap and let the level of liquid fall until 10 cm³ has been removed.
11 15 cm³
12 90 cm³
13 51.22 g

## What are they doing wrong? (PB page 12)

Figure 1.15 on PB page 11 can be used as a trigger to these questions. The idea of safety may be introduced by asking the pupils to say what in the picture they consider to be unsafe behaviour. After the picture has been discussed, the pupils can then read the text and answer the questions.

1 Paul ran in the laboratory and did not put his bag out of the way. Jenny should have tied her hair back. Brian should have worn eye protection and should not have looked down the test-tube. He should not have pointed the test-tube at Paul. Jane should not have been eating in the laboratory. Jenny should have asked the teacher if she was not sure about setting up the apparatus. Angela should not have shouted in the laboratory. Paul should not have picked up broken glass with his fingers. Paul should not have been making up his own experiment without checking it with the teacher.
2 The stool was not put out of the way. The bench-tops had not been cleaned.

# INTRODUCING CHEMISTRY

## Laboratory rules (PB page 12)

**For discussion**
**Entering and leaving the laboratory** Running can lead to collisions between people and furniture, which in turn may cause people to fall or knock against apparatus and damage it or cause it to fall too.

If bags are left out on the laboratory floor they become obstacles which people can fall over.

The stools are out of the way under the bench and are not obstacles when people are walking about during their practical work.

Any chemicals left on the bench-top may come into contact with skin, clothes and books, where they may cause damage.

**General behaviour** Running can lead to collisions between people and furniture, which in turn may cause people to fall or knock against apparatus and damage it or cause it to fall too.

Food and drink may become contaminated with chemicals in the laboratory. These chemicals may be harmful when ingested.

Noise can cause people to be distracted from their work. This can lead to inaccurate measurements and to poor attention being paid to practical procedures such as heating apparatus or pouring liquids, which could lead to injury.

**Preparing to do practical work** Long hair could catch fire if it swings in front of a Bunsen burner flame.

Lab coats protect normal school clothing. They should be buttoned up to protect the wearer's clothes from splashes and burns when the wearer is performing experiments.

Some substances may 'spit' when they are heated and hazardous chemicals may be splashed when they are poured if a great deal of care is not taken. The eye protection protects the surface of the eyes, which are more delicate than the skin.

**During experiments** Chemicals taking part in reactions or being heated may shoot out of the top of the tube if great care is not taken and may hit anyone in the way or looking down the tube.

The teacher needs to know of breakages and spillages so he or she can warn other pupils and arrange for these hazards to be removed.

If the correct procedure is not followed, unsafe situations may develop where heating may cause violent chemical reactions, or the reactions will not take place at all.

The teacher knows the hazards when experiments are being devised and can assess if the procedure is safe.

If gas supplies are not used sensibly there is a danger of fire and explosions.

If water supplies are not used sensibly there is a danger of flooding and of affecting electricity supplies.

If electrical supplies are not used sensibly there is a danger of electrocution and of fires.

## Warning signs (PB page 12)

14 a) breaks down a substance
   b) causes a rash or itching
   c) easily catches fire
   d) produces rays we cannot see that can damage the tissues of our bodies
   e) poisonous

## End of chapter question (PB page 14)

1 a) Tie your hair back if it is long and wear a lab coat. Put your stool under the bench when you begin your practical work. Do not shout, eat or drink in the laboratory. Wear eye protection when heating anything or using hazardous chemicals. Do not look down test-tubes or point them at anyone. Report any breakages or spillages to your teacher at once. Check with your teacher if you are not sure about a procedure or if you have planned an experiment. Use the gas, water and electricity supplies sensibly. Clean your bench when you have finished and leave the stool under the bench.

   b) When reading the volume of a liquid in a measuring cylinder make sure that the base of the cylinder is on a flat surface. Put your eye level with the surface of the liquid in the middle of the cylinder or a burette. When reading the volume of a gas in a syringe make sure you can see where the edge of the plunger comes to rest and read the volume at this point. When using a thermometer keep the bulb in the substance you are investigating while you read its temperature – do not take the thermometer out of a liquid and then read the temperature.

# End of chapter test (WORKSHEET 1.3, TRB page 7)

1. Stand the measuring cylinder so that it is flat on the bench. Pour in the liquid without splashing or spilling, put your eye in line with the meniscus and read from the centre of the meniscus. Add more liquid or pour some out until the correct volume is reached.
2. Place a beaker or conical flask under the burette and turn the tap. Allow the liquid to flow out until 15 cm³ has been removed, and then close the tap.
3. a) As far in as it will go – at the 0 cm³ mark on the scale.
   b) It moves back up the syringe.
   c) The syringe stops moving.
   d) By reading the scale at the place where the plunger comes to rest.
4. a) Add liquid to the beaker until the combined mass of the beaker and the liquid is 130 g.
   b) Put the beaker on the pan and move the tare to set the reading to zero, then add the liquid until a reading of 70 g is displayed.
5. a) 24°C
   b) The meniscus of the mercury goes down the side of the tube and the meniscus of water goes up.
6. The clinical thermometer has a narrow bend in the tube through which the mercury moves. This bend prevents the mercury moving back into the bulb. The mercury can be returned to the bulb by shaking the thermometer. A laboratory thermometer does not have a bend in it, so the mercury can return to the bulb as soon as the temperature falls.
7.
8. a) wear eye protection
   b) harmful or irritant
   c) toxic
   d) corrosive
9.

## IT input

Hall of Fame:
- Robert Bunsen, PB page 7
- Justus von Liebig, PB page 8

# Activities

## Activity 1.1 Identifying apparatus

### *Apparatus* (PB page 6)

This activity will help pupils identify the different pieces of apparatus and help them transfer their observational skills from the Pupil's Book to the laboratory situation. The pupils are presented with three groups of apparatus in turn in a circus and asked to identify as many pieces as possible without using their books. They may use their books later to check their answers or revise their work. Some pieces (test-tube, boiling tube and clamp and stand) are presented twice – once together and once apart to check the pupils' ability to identify them when apart.

**Preparation**

One or more sets of labelled apparatus in groups A, B and C. The apparatus may be labelled A1, A2 etc.

- Group A: 250 cm³ beaker, gauze, delivery tube, round bottomed flask, test-tube, clamp
- Group B: test-tube, boiling tube, Bunsen burner, tripod, clamp and stand, thermometer
- Group C: filter funnel, conical flask, separating funnel, flat bottomed flask, boiling tube, stand

# INTRODUCING CHEMISTRY

## Activity 1.2 Investigating lathers

### *Measuring volumes of liquids* (PB page 2)

WORKSHEET 1.1 Looking at lather (TRB page 5)
This activity allows the development of skills in using the measuring cylinder, burette and stop clock. It also introduces two unfamiliar chemicals and a familiar one in an unusual context. The pupils should be taken through the worksheet and introduced to all the equipment before they are set to try the investigation. They should also construct a table for their results before they begin their work.

The activity could be extended into a study of hard and soft water at the teacher's discretion.

**Preparation**
- For each class group: burette of soap solution set up in a clamp and stand, measuring cylinder, conical flask and stopper, stop clock
- Chemicals: 0.005 M solutions of calcium chloride, sodium chloride and magnesium chloride, distilled water

**Safety**
- Eye protection must be worn.
- Take care when setting up the burettes of soap solution.
- Soap solutions are often made up in ethanol, and therefore, may be flammable.

## Activity 1.3 Investigating how different volumes of water heat up

### *Bunsen burner* (PB pages 7 and 84), *Laboratory rules* (PB page 9) and *What are they doing wrong?* (PB page 11)

WORKSHEET 1.2 How do different volumes of water heat up? (TRB page 6)
The Bunsen burner may be introduced with the other laboratory apparatus and the pupils may look at the section in Chapter 7 which features it before the sections on air in that chapter are studied.

This activity allows an assessment of the pupils' developing practical skills with a range of apparatus. Although safety must always be stressed before practical work, this activity also allows the pupils to assess their performance of safe practice against the laboratory rules and the section 'What are they doing wrong?'. Depending on the pupils' previous experience they may be set the activity as a challenge and use the investigation skill sheets, or they may use Worksheet 1.2. If the worksheet is used the pupils should be taken through the work and should construct a table for their results before they start the practical work.

While the pupils are waiting for the beaker to cool down they could construct graphs of their results.

**Preparation**
- For each class group: 250 cm$^3$ beaker, Bunsen burner, heatproof mat, tripod, gauze, stop clock, measuring cylinder, thermometer

**Safety**
- Eye protection must be worn.
- Make sure that the tripods have cooled down before clearing them away.

## Activity 1.4 Comparing the masses of solids

### *Measuring the mass of a solid or liquid* (PB page 3)

This activity tests the pupils' skill in using the top pan balance, helps them to estimate and provides data for Activity 2.1 in Chapter 2, which may be done at the same time as this activity.

The pupils are given blocks of different materials and asked to find the mass of each one. After the mass of the first block has been found the pupils should estimate the masses of the other blocks before they weigh them, and construct a table of their estimated and actual results.

**Preparation**
- For each class group: blocks of wood, wax, plastic, steel, aluminium and lead
- Top loading balance

**Safety**
- Wash hands after handling lead.

# WORKSHEET 1.1 *Looking at lather*

 Eye protection must be worn

 The soap solution may be flammable

Carry out the following procedure with **a)** distilled water, **b)** calcium chloride solution, **c)** sodium chloride solution, **d)** magnesium chloride solution.

1. Measure out 25 cm$^3$ of the first of the liquids listed above into the measuring cylinder.
2. Pour the liquid into a conical flask.
3. Add 0.5 cm$^3$ of soap solution from the burette.
4. Put the stopper in the flask.
5. Shake the flask and allow the liquid to stand for 2 minutes. Then observe the development of the lather and record your result.
6. Repeat steps 3, 4 and 5 until the lather covers the whole of the water surface for 2 minutes.
7. Rinse the flask out with tap water then distilled water.

Repeat with the other liquids.
Construct a table of your results in the space below.

# INTRODUCING CHEMISTRY

# WORKSHEET 1.2  *How do different volumes of water heat up?*

 Eye protection must be worn

! Make sure that the tripod has cooled down before clearing it away

1. Measure out 50 cm³ of water.
2. Pour it into the beaker.
3. Take the temperature of the water and record it.
4. Put the beaker on the tripod and gauze and heat it with the Bunsen burner.
5. Record the temperature every 30 seconds for 5 minutes.
6. Allow the beaker to cool and then empty it.
7. Repeat steps 1 to 6 with **a)** 100 cm³ of water and **b)** 150 cm³ of water.
8. Predict the result for heating 200 cm³ of water and then test your prediction.

Construct a table of your results in the space below.

# WORKSHEET 1.3   *End of chapter test*

1. How would you use a measuring cylinder to measure a volume of a liquid?
2. A burette contains 40 cm$^3$ of a liquid. How would you measure out 15 cm$^3$?
3. A syringe is being used in a chemical reaction to measure the amount of gas produced.
   a) Where should the plunger in the syringe be placed at the beginning of the experiment?
   b) What happens to the plunger as the chemical reaction takes place?
   c) How can you tell when the reaction has finished?
   d) How would you find the volume of gas produced by the reaction?
4. You have a beaker of mass 60 g and you need to weigh out 70 g of a liquid. How will you do this using a machine that a) does not have a tare, b) has a tare?
5. a) What temperature does this thermometer show?

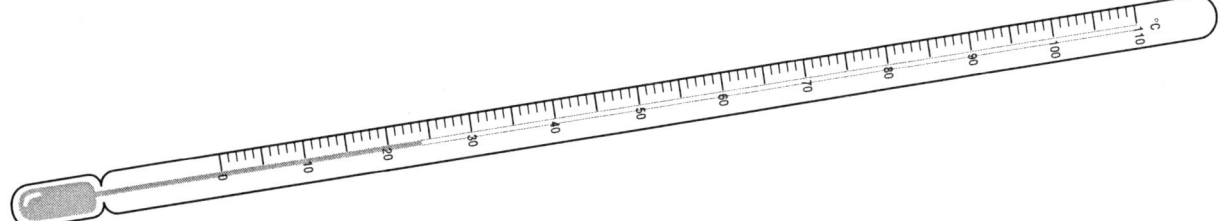

   b) How is the meniscus of the mercury different from the meniscus of water?
6. How is a clinical thermometer different from a thermometer you may use in experiments in the laboratory?
7. Draw a diagram of a conical flask on a gauze supported by a tripod.
8. What are these warning signs?

a)    b)    c)    d)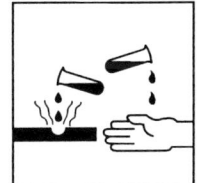

9. Draw the sign which warns you that a substance is highly flammable.

# 2 The world of matter

## Answers

### Matter everywhere (PB page 15)

**For discussion** If there were no solids the surface of the Earth would be covered by water but the atmosphere could still exist. There would be no sea bed, just water right though the planet. Life forms would have to be similar to jellyfish, but softer and capable of flowing. Life forms having bones and shells could not exist.

If there were no liquids the planet would be covered by land. It could have an atmosphere. It could be similar to Mars (although the presence of water has been detected there). There would be no life forms as we know them as water is needed for life on Earth.

If there were no gases the planet would be covered in land and seas but there would be no atmosphere. There could be some life forms in the seas which could have bones and shells. As liquids evaporated from their surface any vapour escaping from the surface would have to be removed. In time all the liquid would evaporate.

It would not be possible for us to live in any of the imaginary worlds because we need air and water and are made from parts of the body which are solid.

### Properties of matter (PB page 16)

1

| Solid | Liquid | Gas |
|---|---|---|
| definite mass | definite mass | definite mass |
| definite volume | definite volume | volume can change |
| definite shape | no definite shape | no definite shape |
| high density | high density | low density |
| hard to make flow | easy to make flow | easy to make flow |
| hard to compress | hard to compress | easy to compress |

2 a) All states of matter have a definite mass.
   b) The volume of solids and liquids remains the same but the volume of a gas can change. Solids remain the same shape but liquids and gases can change shape. Solids and liquids have high densities and gases have low densities. Solids are hard to make flow but liquids and gases flow easily. Solids and liquids are hard to compress but gases compress easily.

3 a) $0.65 \text{ g/cm}^3$  b) $0.8 \text{ g/cm}^3$
   c) $0.0013 \text{ g/cm}^3$

### The first ideas about matter (PB page 19)

1 They could use fire to change one material into another.
2 The Greeks did not try to test their ideas with experiments but tried to explain them with more ideas.
3 Thales saw water change into ice and ice into water and saw water boil away into the air and water condense out of the air.
4 earth
5 hot and dry
6 a) earth (solid), water (steam comes out when it burns), fire (flames come out when it gets hot)
   b) water (oil is runny), fire (flames come out when it gets hot)
   c) earth (solid), water (melts into a liquid when hot), fire (glows when red or white hot)
7 Fire escapes in the flame. The candle appears to be made of the earth element which changes into the water element. But when the candle is burnt up, nothing is left, suggesting that it contained the air element which has escaped.
8 Because the ideas matched what people could see and they believed in them. Scientific experiments were not devised during this time to test the ideas.

### The changing state of water (PB pages 22 and 23)

4 dew, frost
5

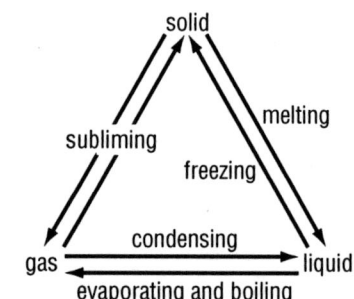

… ANSWERS

## Particles of matter (PB page 24)

**6** Strong forces hold the particles together in a three-dimensional structure in solids. In liquids, the forces that hold the particles together are weaker and the particles can move over each other.

**7** The particles in a gas can move away from each other and move in any direction. In a liquid, the particles slide over each other in one general direction when the liquid is poured.

## When matter changes state (PB page 26)

**8** When a solid substance melts, the particles vibrate more strongly and eventually slide over each other. When a liquid substance evaporates, the particles with the highest energy near the liquid surface break through the surface and escape into the air.

**9** Boiling occurs when a liquid changes into a gas at a temperature called the boiling point. The fastest moving particles escape from the liquid and form bubbles which eventually escape from the liquid and the gas they contain mixes with the air. Sublimation occurs when a solid turns into a gas. The particles in the solid separate and form a gas when they receive enough heat energy. Sublimation also occurs when a gas turns into a solid. When the gas particles are cooled they form the orderly arrangement of a solid and vibrate about one position.

**10** The substance is cooled down and the particles lose energy in both freezing and condensation.

## Pressure (PB page 27)

**11** increasing the temperature of the gas, or squashing the gas into a smaller space while keeping its temperature the same

**12 a)** It is reduced.
**b)** The particles bounce off the walls less frequently as they spend more time moving through the space of the larger container.

## Pressure and changes of state (PB page 28)

**13** All three planets have an atmosphere. Below the atmosphere of the Earth are liquid and solid surfaces; below the atmospheres of the other two planets is a liquid surface. Much of these two planets is made of liquid, while much of the Earth is made of the mantle which is more solid. All three planets have a core. The Earth's core is made of iron while the cores of the other two planets are made of rock.

## Atmospheric pressure (PB page 29)

**14** The water would boil at a lower temperature. There is less air pressure on the surface of the liquid, so particles with high energy near the surface can leave the water more easily than at normal atmospheric pressure.

## Structure of matter (PB page 30)

**1** The paper can become as small as the pupils' fingers will allow.
**2** The atoms had a rough surface with jagged pieces which interlocked together to make the rigid material of stones and the ground.
**3** Hero's idea was very similar to the kinetic theory of gases.
**4** Boyle wrote down descriptions of his experiments very carefully so they could be repeated.
**5** Gases can be converted into liquids by condensation and into solids either by freezing the liquid that forms from the gas or in some cases, such as with sulphur, by sublimation.

## Diffusion (PB page 31)

**15 a)** b) c)

## Identifying substances (PB page 31)

**16 a)** nitrogen, ammonia
**b)** nitrogen, ammonia, bromine
**17** iron

Chemistry Now! 11–14 Teacher's Resource Book

# THE WORLD OF MATTER

## End of chapter questions (PB page 32)

1 This will depend on the shoe but the materials may include leather, porous plastic materials, cotton, wool, cord, steel pins.
2 The particles in the ice are bound together strongly and vibrate about a fixed point. As the ice melts the particles move further apart then slide over each other to form a liquid. The particles with the highest energy near the surface of the water break through the surface and escape into the air.
3 When air is pumped into a bicycle tyre more particles are squashed into the tyre. They join the others in colliding with the inner wall of the tyre, and the pressure rises.

## End of chapter test (WORKSHEET 2.1, TRB page 14)

1 a) gas   b) solid   c) liquid
2 8 g/cm$^3$
3 18 cm$^3$
4 1800 g
5 a) melting   b) evaporating   c) condensing
   d) freezing
6 a)   b)   c)

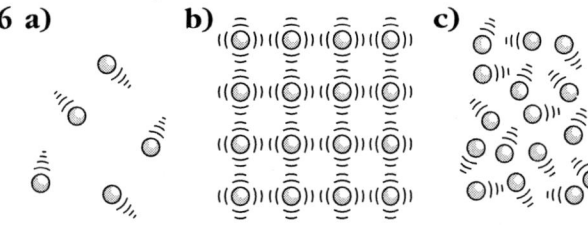

7 a) boiling   b) freezing   c) condensing
8 a) The particles change from staying close together in one place and vibrating to moving far apart from each other and moving in different directions.
   b) subliming

## IT input

Hall of Fame:

- Thales, PB page 19
- Democritus, PB page 30
- Hero, PB page 30
- Robert Boyle, PB page 30
- James Clerk Maxwell, PB page 30
- Ludwig Boltzmann, PB page 30

## Activities

### Activity 2.1 The density of solids

*Properties of matter* (PB page 15)

The concept of density is mentioned in the chemistry course and developed more fully in the physics course. This activity builds on the skills in Activity 1.4 and provides an experience in calculating density to supplement the work in the physics course.

The pupils measure the dimensions of the blocks and find their volumes, then calculate the density of each one by dividing its mass by its volume. They present their results as a list of the materials, starting with the most dense material at the top of the list.

**Preparation**

- For each class group: blocks of wood, wax, plastic, steel, aluminium and lead
- Top pan balance, rulers

**Safety**

- Wash hands after handling lead.

### Activity 2.2 Investigating the melting point of ice

*Changing states* (PB page 20)

The pupils are asked to record the temperature of ice in a beaker and to predict how the temperature of the ice and water will change as the beaker is slowly warmed.

The pupils then perform the experiment and check their prediction, with the result that all the ice melts before the temperature of the water begins to rise. This observation can be developed further in the physics course when internal energy is considered.

**Preparation**

- For each class group: 250 cm$^3$ beaker, Bunsen burner, heatproof mat, tripod, gauze, thermometer, ice

**Safety**

- Eye protection must be worn.
- Make sure that the tripods have cooled down before clearing them away.

# ACTIVITIES

## Activity 2.3 Investigating the melting point of naphthalene

*Changing states* (PB page 20)

The pupils can follow up the investigation in Activity 2.2 by heating a test-tube containing naphthalene in a water bath, then removing the test-tube from the bath, inserting a thermometer in it and recording the temperature every 30 seconds as the naphthalene cools.

Prior to the investigation the use and making of a water bath with a beaker, tripod and gauze should be discussed and the pupils shown how to use a test-tube holder correctly.

**Preparation**
- For each class group: Bunsen burner, heatproof mat, tripod, gauze, beaker, test-tube about a quarter full of naphthalene, ceramic wool, test-tube holder, test-tube rack, thermometer, stop clock

**Safety**
- Eye protection must be worn.
- Some employers may not permit the use of naphthalene. If naphthalene cannot be used, then cetyl alcohol or stearic acid can be substituted as alternatives.
- Naphthalene is toxic, irritating to the eyes and skin, and possibly carcinogenic. A loose plug of ceramic wool must be inserted into the test-tubes to prevent naphthalene vapour escaping.
- Make sure that the tripods have cooled down before clearing them away.

## Activity 2.4 Heating sulphur

*Changing states* (PB page 20)

Only perform this activity if you feel you can carefully supervise all pupils in the class. This activity can be used to introduce the pupils to the use of a spatula and the weighing out of a solid and to reinforce the use of a test-tube holder.

The pupils weigh out 1 g of sulphur and put it in a test-tube. A loose plug of mineral wool should then be placed in the top of the test-tube to minimise the risk of sulphur vapour escaping and catching fire. Pupils should heat the sulphur *gently* until it melts, and record their observations. The pupils then put the test-tube of sulphur in the test-tube rack to watch the sulphur solidify.

**Preparation**
- For each class group: spatula, test-tube, test-tube holder, test-tube rack, mineral wool, Bunsen burner, heatproof mat
- Chemicals: jar of crushed roll sulphur
- One or more top pan balances
- Access to a fume cupboard

**Safety**
- Eye protection must be worn.
- Heat sulphur in a fume cupboard – sulphur dioxide is toxic and may induce an asthma attack and be irritating to the eyes.
- Sulphur should not be heated strongly. It will ignite if it is overheated.

## Activity 2.5 Sublimation of carbon dioxide

*Sublimation* (PB page 21)

This may be done as a class demonstration with pupil participation. The pupils observe dry ice warming and are asked to predict what might happen if some were placed in a balloon. The equivalent of two teaspoons of dry ice is then placed in a balloon. (The neck of the balloon will need to be stretched wide to allow the ice to enter.) The balloon is then flattened to remove the air and the neck is quickly tied. The pupils can then be asked to estimate the change in volume of the balloon when all the carbon dioxide has turned to gas. The volume of gas is about 600 times larger than the volume of the solid.

**Preparation**
- For the teacher: solid carbon dioxide (dry ice), teaspoon, balloon

**Safety**
- Eye protection must be worn.
- Handle dry ice with protective gloves.

## Activity 2.6 Particles and matter

*Particles of matter* (PB page 23) and *Pressure* (PB page 26)

This can be introduced as an exercise in scientific modelling.

# THE WORLD OF MATTER

Ask the pupils to demonstrate **a)** how particles are arranged in a solid (they should tip the tray so the marbles form rows), **b)** how particles move when a liquid flows (they should turn the tipped tray so the marbles flow to a new position), **c)** how the particles move in a gas (they should keep the tray flat and shake it so the marbles move about, hitting one another and the sides of the tray). In **c)**, the pupils can also be asked to identify those particles which are creating a pressure on the walls of a container (they are those hitting the sides of the tray).

**Preparation**
- For each class group: small tray with enough marbles to make three rows when the tray is tipped
- Some pupils might exhibit behavioural problems if presented with a tray of marbles. You may prefer to use just one set of equipment and let one group of pupils demonstrate to the whole class.

## Activity 2.7 The effects of gas particles on smoke

*Particles of matter* (PB page 23) and *Solid/gas mixtures* (PB page 34)

Introduce the idea that smoke is made of solid particles which are larger than the particles in the gas. Ask the pupils how they could introduce a smoke particle into their model (they should agree to add a larger marble) and to predict what would happen to this particle (it would be moved about in a random way by the gas particles hitting it). The pupils then introduce a larger marble into their trays and test their prediction.

The activity can be concluded by allowing the pupils to view a smoke cell through the microscope and match their observations with their model of the movement of smoke.

**Preparation**
- For each class group: small tray with enough marbles to make three rows when the tray is tipped, one larger marble
- For the class demonstration: microscope set up with a smoke cell

## Activity 2.8 Diffusion of copper sulphate

*Diffusion* (PB page 31) and *Solutions* (PB page 35)

Present the pupils with a beaker of copper sulphate solution, a gas jar, funnel and a glass tube and ask them to devise a way of setting up a layer of copper sulphate solution below a layer of water. The pupils should then work out that the water is put in first and the layer of denser copper sulphate solution is built up below it by pouring it through the funnel and tube to the bottom of the jar. If this is done carefully the two liquids do not mix.

Ask the pupils to devise a way of measuring the rate of diffusion of the copper sulphate solution through the water and arrange for there to be supervised access to the laboratory after the lesson to make measurements.

**Preparation**
- For each class group: beaker containing a 2 M solution of copper sulphate, gas jar, filter funnel, wide glass tube

**Safety**
- Eye protection must be worn.
- Copper sulphate as a solid and in 2 M solution is harmful – remove any from the skin by washing immediately.

## Activity 2.9 Diffusion of iodine solution

*Diffusion* (PB page 31) and *Solutions* (PB page 35)

Let the pupils set up a Petri dish of cold water on a piece of graph paper. When the water is still the teacher should use forceps to add a small crystal of iodine to the water in the centre of the dish and let the pupils watch it dissolve and time its diffusion through the water. Ask the pupils to predict what would happen if the experiment was repeated with warm water. If possible they should test their prediction. The pupils should find that the iodine diffuses more quickly in the warm water.

# ACTIVITIES

**Preparation**
- For each class group: Petri dish, graph paper, stop clock
- For the teacher: bottle of iodine crystals, forceps

**Safety**
- Eye protection must be worn.
- Iodine as a solid and in solutions stronger than 1 M is harmful by inhalation or skin contact and may be irritating to the eyes. Iodine solid can cause burns to the skin if not washed off immediately.

## Activity 2.10 Investigating salt and water

### *Testing for purity* (PB page 32) and *Solutions* (PB page 35)

Ask the pupils to investigate how salt in water affects its boiling point. The pupils should first find the boiling point of water as recorded by their thermometer. The variation in accuracy of thermometers and the need to check the boiling point with the apparatus used in the experiment can be discussed. The pupils then make a salt solution and find that its boiling point is higher than that of pure water.

If Activity 2.3 has been performed and the pupils are competent in the use of the water bath the investigation could be extended to devising a way of finding the boiling point of a small sample of the flammable liquid ethanol.

**Preparation**
- For each class group: boiling tube, clamp and stand, thermometer, Bunsen burner, heatproof mat, spatula, stirring rod, beaker
- Chemicals: dish of salt
- For the extension practical each class group will need: thermostatically-controlled water bath, test-tube with small amount of ethanol present, thermometer

**Safety**
- Eye protection must be worn.
- Ethanol is highly flammable and irritating to the eyes. Turn off all Bunsen burners before bringing the ethanol tubes into the laboratory.
- Mercury is toxic, but there is no immediate problem – it only works slowly. You need access to a spill kit in case of thermometer breakages.

# THE WORLD OF MATTER

## WORKSHEET 2.1  *End of chapter test*

1. Which state of matter **a)** compresses easily, **b)** has a fixed shape, **c)** flows but has a fixed volume?
2. What is the density of a substance which has a volume of 100 cm³ and a mass of 800 g?
3. A substance has a density of 9 g/cm³ and a mass of 162 g. What is its volume?
4. A substance has a volume of 300 cm³ and a density of 6 g/cm³. What is its mass?
5. What is the name of the process in which
   **a)** a solid turns into a liquid,
   **b)** a liquid turns into a gas over a range of temperatures,
   **c)** a gas cools and turns into a liquid,
   **d)** a liquid turns into a solid?
6. Draw diagrams to show how particles are arranged in **a)** a gas, **b)** a solid, **c)** a liquid.
7. In which process do
   **a)** fast moving particles form bubbles in a hot liquid,
   **b)** particles moving over each other stop in one place and vibrate,
   **c)** fast moving particles slow down, come closer and slide over each other?
8. **a)** Describe how the action of a particle in a substance changes when the substance changes from a solid into a gas.
   **b)** What is the name of the process you have described in a)?

## WORKSHEET 2.1  *End of chapter test*

1. Which state of matter **a)** compresses easily, **b)** has a fixed shape, **c)** flows but has a fixed volume?
2. What is the density of a substance which has a volume of 100 cm³ and a mass of 800 g?
3. A substance has a density of 9 g/cm³ and a mass of 162 g. What is its volume?
4. A substance has a volume of 300 cm³ and a density of 6 g/cm³. What is its mass?
5. What is the name of the process in which
   **a)** a solid turns into a liquid,
   **b)** a liquid turns into a gas over a range of temperatures,
   **c)** a gas cools and turns into a liquid,
   **d)** a liquid turns into a solid?
6. Draw diagrams to show how particles are arranged in **a)** a gas, **b)** a solid, **c)** a liquid.
7. In which process do
   **a)** fast moving particles form bubbles in a hot liquid,
   **b)** particles moving over each other stop in one place and vibrate,
   **c)** fast moving particles slow down, come closer and slide over each other?
8. **a)** Describe how the action of a particle in a substance changes when the substance changes from a solid into a gas.
   **b)** What is the name of the process you have described in a)?

# 3 Separation of mixtures

# Answers

## Mixtures and compounds (PB page 33)

1

|  | Mixture | Compound |
|---|---|---|
| Amount of different substances | varies | fixed |
| Formed by chemical reaction? | no | yes |
| Change in heat energy occurs on formation? | no | yes |
| Properties of substance | same as substances in mixture | different from substances in mixture |
| Separation by physical means? | yes | no |
| Separation by chemical means? | no | yes |

## Solutions (PB pages 35 and 36)

2 A solvent is a substance which dissolves a substance in it. A solute is a substance which dissolves in a solvent.

3 A substance that is soluble in water dissolves in it and a substance that is insoluble in water does not dissolve in it.

4 An immiscible substance is one that does not dissolve in a particular solvent. An emulsion is made up of two immiscible liquids.

## Solubility (PB page 36)

5 The solubility of sodium chloride rises a very small amount with an increase in temperature and then falls. The solubility of copper sulphate increases slowly at first but more rapidly between 70 and 80°C. The solubility of potassium nitrate is much greater than the other two substances at higher temperatures.

6 The solubility increases from about 48 g/100 g to about 88 g/100 g.

## Liquids and gases in solvents (PB page 37)

7 When the water is cold the solubility is higher than when the water is warm.

## Separating mixtures (PB page 38)

8 oil, a range of chemicals and compressed air

## Separating an insoluble solid/liquid mixture (PB page 40)

9 a) Filtration. The filter has small holes in it which the water can pass through but the fine sand cannot. The sand is left behind in the paper.

b) Decanting. When the mixture is poured the heavy weight of the gravel keeps it at the bottom of the container.

c) Centrifuge and decanting. The small particles are forced down to the bottom of the tubes as the tubes spin round. They form a sediment. The water may then be poured away by decanting, leaving the sediment at the bottom of the tube.

## Separating a solute from a solute/solvent mixture (PB page 42)

10 Yes

## Separating a solvent from a solute/solvent mixture (PB page 44)

11 The walls of the Liebig condenser do not get hot, so more vapour can condense there. The walls do not get hot because the heat from the vapour is removed by cold water passing through the jacket around the condenser tube.

## Separating two miscible liquids (PB page 45)

12 Because alcohol was boiling out of the mixture during this time.

Chemistry Now! 11–14 Teacher's Resource Book

# SEPARATION OF MIXTURES

13 100°C – the water remaining in the flask would start to boil.

14 The ethanol/water mixture is poured into the flask and the flask is then heated. The first beaker is put under the end of the condenser tube. When the temperature reaches 78°C ethanol vapour enters the condenser, cools and forms a liquid, which is collected in the beaker. The thermometer must be watched carefully for any sign of the temperature starting to rise. As soon as it starts to rise, the beaker is replaced by a second beaker and water is collected.

## End of chapter question (PB page 46)

1 The mixture of sand and salty water would first be filtered to remove the sand and then the salty water would be distilled. The water would be collected after it has condensed and the salt would be left behind in the flask.

## End of chapter test (Worksheet 3.2, TRB page 22)

1 **a)** no **b)** yes
2 statements **ii)** and **iii)**
3 It is formed by tiny particles which float in a liquid and make it cloudy, e.g. clay in water.
4 a mixture of a solid and a gas
5 **a)** The fatty oil does not dissolve in water.
  **b)** an emulsion
6 **a)** heat the water
  **b) i)** water **ii)** the mixture of salt and water **iii)** salt
7 **a)** To separate a solid with large particles from the liquid. The solid forms a sediment at the bottom of the container and the liquid is carefully poured off so that the sediment is not disturbed.
  **b)** To separate a solid with tiny particles from a liquid. The same amount of mixture is put in a pair of test-tubes placed opposite each other in the centrifuge. The machine is then switched on and the particles settle to the bottom of the tubes.
8 They separate out because they travel at different speeds through the paper as the liquid spreads out.

9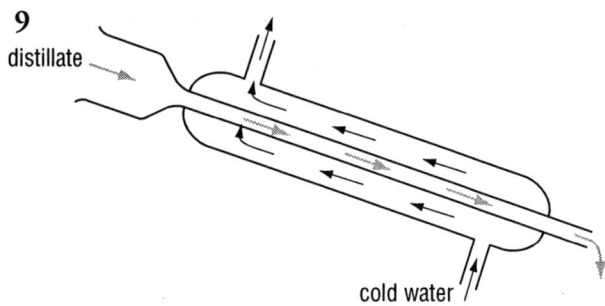

10 **a)** liquid **ii)** **b)** fractional distillation
11 **a)** To separate two immiscible liquids where one floats on top of the other.
   **b)** The mixture is poured into the funnel and allowed to settle so that two layers of liquid form. Then the tap is opened to let out the lower layer of liquid. The upper layer stays in the funnel and is poured out separately.

## IT input

Hall of Fame:

- Eduard Buchner, PB page 40

## Activities

### Activity 3.1 Investigating the dissolving of sugar

*Solubility* (PB page 36)

Ask the pupils to devise a way of testing the effect of particle size on the speed at which sugar dissolves. In their answers look for divisions of three or more size groups in a certain volume of water and the dissolving of equal masses of sugar.

**Preparation**
- For each class group: large lumps of sugar, mortar and pestle, beaker, measuring cylinder, glass rod, spatula, stop clock
- Top pan balance

**Safety**
- Warn pupils against tasting due to the risk of contamination.

### Activity 3.2 Investigating solubility

*Solubility* (PB page 36)

Ask the pupils to compare the solubility of salt and copper sulphate. This should lead them to try and dissolve equal masses of solute in equal masses of water. Look for pupils also investigating the effect of heat on the solubility of the substances.

Demonstrate the safe heating of a solution in a test-tube with a Bunsen burner and look for the pupils' discovery that salt is more soluble than copper sulphate in cool water but that the solubility of salt hardly increases with temperature while the solubility of copper sulphate increases with a rise in temperature and exceeds the solubility of salt at higher temperatures (over 60°C).

Look for the pupils discovering that a hot concentrated solution of copper sulphate forms crystals as it cools.

**Preparation**
- For each class group: two Pyrex test-tubes, test-tube rack, test-tube holder, Bunsen burner, heatproof mat, thermometer, measuring cylinder
- Chemicals: sodium chloride crystals, copper sulphate crystals
- Top pan balance

**Safety**
- Eye protection must be worn.
- Copper sulphate as a solid and in a solution stronger than 1 M is harmful – remove any from the skin by washing immediately.

## Activity 3.3 Soil studies

*Separating a solid/solid mixture* (PB page 37) and *Separating an insoluble solid/liquid mixture* (PB page 39)

1 Ask the pupils to assess a gauze as a soil filter. Ask them to place a sample of soil on the gauze and then gently shake the gauze. They should give a brief description of the result then try step 2 before they complete their answer.

2 Ask the pupils to stir up a sample of soil with water and then let it settle. Let the pupils describe what they see and look for the use of the words 'suspension' and 'sediment' in their answers. Ask them to draw a labelled diagram of the mixture after it has settled for five minutes. Let them compare the contents of the soil revealed in this experiment with step 1 so that they can assess how good the gauze is at separating particles in soil.

3 As an extension, let the pupils add a spatula of slaked lime to the water and ask them to record their observations. The flocculation of the clay particles causes the water to clear and a layer of large particles to form above the silt.

Develop the idea of how lime helps improve the soil by making a model of soil with small particles and large particles. The small-particle model is made by placing 30 small discs on a piece of 1 mm squared graph paper and assessing the spaces between the discs by counting the squares that can be seen in the gaps. The large-particle soil model is made by using large discs on the graph paper. The pupils should work out a relationship between particle size and gaps between particles, and the speed of drainage and the availability of oxygen to plant roots.

**Preparation**
- For each class group: tripod, gauze, soil sample which includes clay, small gas jar, glass rod, lime, spatula, piece of 1 mm squared graph paper, 30 small cardboard discs (about the size of a 5p piece), 30 large cardboard discs (about the size of a 2p piece)

**Safety**
- Eye protection must be worn.
- Ensure that the soil sample has been collected from an area that is not contaminated by dog faeces, etc.
- Calcium hydroxide is corrosive.

## Activity 3.4 Separating solids from liquids

*Separating an insoluble solid/liquid mixture* (PB page 39)

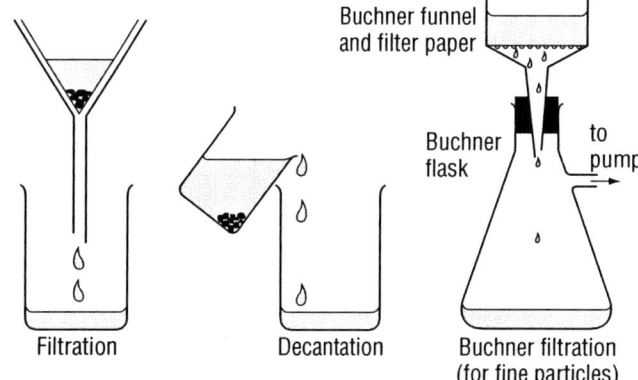

Filtration    Decantation    Buchner filtration (for fine particles)

Chemistry Now! 11–14 Teacher's Resource Book

# SEPARATION OF MIXTURES

This activity will enable students to learn the processes of separating solid matter from a liquid.

The students are presented with three samples of different sized solid particles in water. They may be asked to solve how to separate the solid from the liquid given a range of equipment. This will develop their problem solving and practical skills.

**Preparation**
- For each class group: beakers, filter funnels, Buchner funnels, Buchner flasks, filter paper
- Chemicals: granular zinc, charcoal, iron filings, water

## Activity 3.5 Separation of liquids

### *Separating immiscible liquids* (PB page 45)

Let the pupils add cold cooking oil to water and stir to test for miscibility. Let them compare decanting with the use of a separating funnel as methods of separating the mixture.

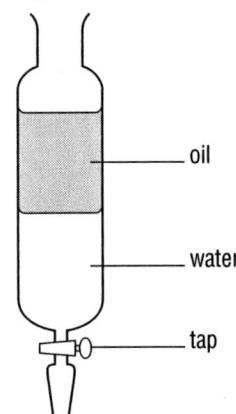

**Preparation**
- For each class group: beakers, separating funnel, stirring rod
- Chemicals: cooking oil, water

## Activity 3.6 Formation of copper sulphate crystals

### *Separating a solute from a solute/solvent mixture* (PB page 41)

The pupils have the opportunity to see crystals of copper sulphate form as the water is evaporated or the solution is cooled. This activity could also be carried out after the neutralisation reactions in Chapter 6, Activity 6.3.

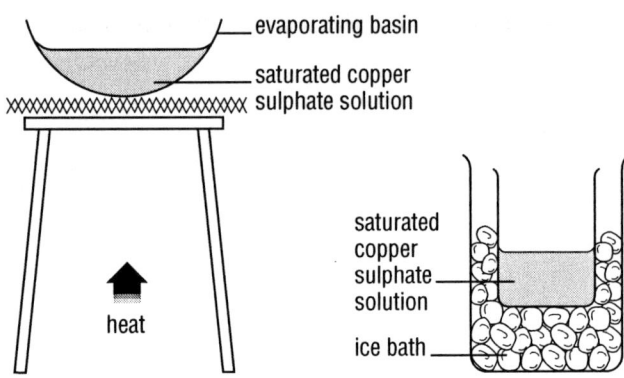

**Preparation**
- For each class group: Bunsen burner, heatproof mat, gauze, tripod, evaporating basin, ice bath
- Chemicals: saturated solution of copper sulphate

**Safety**
- Eye protection must be worn.
- Saturated copper sulphate solution is harmful – remove any by washing immediately.
- Make sure that the tripods have cooled down before clearing them away.

## Activity 3.7 Separating mixtures

### *Separating a solid/solid mixture* (PB page 37)

This activity allows the separation of a mixture of solids using the differences in their chemical properties. It is useful to perform this as a practical investigation, but it may be a good idea to do this after the students have become familiar with the properties of the elements as studied in Chapter 9. The investigation sheets may be used.

The best method of separating a mixture of sand and salt is to place it in water to dissolve the salt, allowing the sand to be filtered. The salt may then be isolated by evaporation of the water.

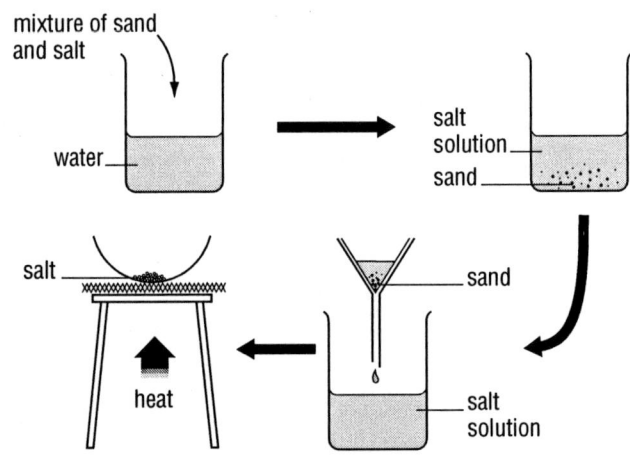

# ACTIVITIES

Separation of the mixture of iodine and salt may be done as a teacher demonstration in a fume cupboard. The separation can be achieved by heating the mixture beneath an inverted watch glass. As the iodine sublimes at a low temperature, it will evaporate and condense back to a solid on the watch glass, as shown in the diagram. Iodine vapour must not be allowed to escape into the laboratory atmosphere.

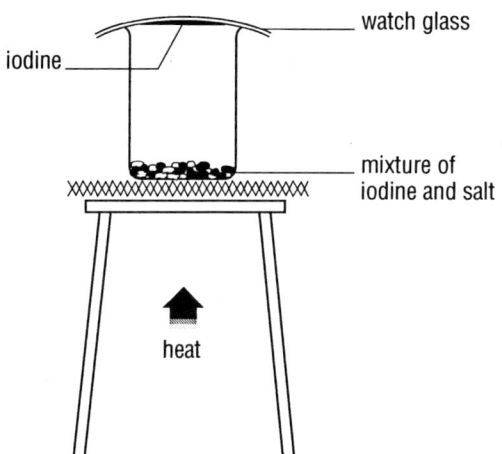

### Preparation
- For each class group: beakers, Bunsen burner, heatproof mat, tripod, gauze, evaporating basin, filter funnel, filter paper, watch glass
- Chemicals: mixture of sand and salt, mixture of iodine and salt

### Safety
- Eye protection must be worn.
- Iodine solid is harmful by inhalation or skin contact and may be irritating to the eyes. It can cause burns to the skin if not washed off immediately.
- Make sure that the tripods have cooled down before clearing them away.

## Activity 3.8 Investigating the separation of chalk from salt

*Filtration* (PB page 39) and *Crystallisation* (PB page 41)

Let the pupils compare the solubility of salt and chalk by putting a spatula of each in a small beaker of water. From their observations ask them to devise a way of separating a mixture of salt and chalk.

### Preparation
- For each class group (to be available but not on display while pupils are making their plan): beaker, filter funnel, clamp and stand, filter paper, evaporating dish, gauze, tripod, Bunsen burner, heatproof mat
- Chemicals: chalk powder, salt, mixture of chalk and salt

### Safety
- Eye protection must be worn.
- Make sure that the tripods have cooled down before clearing them away.

## Activity 3.9 Investigating the purification of rock salt

*Filtration* (PB page 39), *Crystallisation* (PB page 41) and *Sedimentary rock* (PB page 97)

Let the pupils examine pieces of rock salt. Ask them to speculate on how it might have formed.

Ask them to look back through Activities 3.7 and 3.8 and to devise a plan to extract the salt quickly from the sample. You may introduce speed into the process as this is an important factor in producing chemicals for industry. The pupils should respond by planning to grind up the rock salt. When the pupils' plans, which include grinding up, dissolving, filtering and crystallisation have been checked, allow them to carry out their experiments.

Extend by demonstrating how the crystals can be cleaned by washing them with a small amount of distilled water in a filter funnel to remove any impurities, and then show the pupils how to dry the crystals with blotting paper.

### Preparation
- For each class group: mortar and pestle, beaker, glass rod, filter funnel, clamp and stand, evaporating dish, gauze, tripod, Bunsen burner, heatproof mat, two pieces of filter paper, blotting paper
- Chemicals: rock salt, distilled water

### Safety
- Eye protection must be worn.
- Make sure that the tripods have cooled down before clearing them away.

Chemistry Now! 11–14 Teacher's Resource Book

## SEPARATION OF MIXTURES

### Activity 3.10 Is grass really green?

*Chromatography* (PB page 42)

WORKSHEET 3.1 Is grass really green?
(TRB page 21)

This activity could be done when the pupils are studying plants in Chapter 7 'How green plants live' in *Biology Now! 11–14* as a revision of photosynthesis. A simpler activity using water-based inks could be done as an introductory activity as described in the *Chemistry Now! 11–14* Pupil's Book.

The three spots are used here to emphasise the need to repeat experiments when making an investigation.

**Preparation**
- For each class group: beaker, filter paper, scissors, mortar and pestle, small measuring cylinder, ruler, dropping pipette or glass rod, watch glass, grass leaves
- Chemicals: propanone (highly flammable)

**Safety**
- Eye protection must be worn.
- Propanone is highly flammable and harmful to the eyes.

### Activity 3.11 Removing the liquid from ink

*Separating a solvent from a solute/solvent mixture* (PB page 43)

Present the pupils with the apparatus for simple distillation (not assembled) and ask them to devise a plan to separate the solid and liquid parts of the ink. When the pupils' plans have been checked allow them to carry out the investigation and ask them to explain why it works.

**Preparation**
- For each class group: clamp and stand, two boiling tubes, stopper with delivery tube attached, beaker, Bunsen burner, heatproof mat
- Chemicals: ink

**Safety**
- Eye protection must be worn.

# SEPARATION OF MIXTURES

# WORKSHEET 3.1  *Is grass really green?*

 Eye protection must be worn

 Handle propanone with great care – it is highly flammable and harmful to the eyes

1  Cut a piece of filter paper so that it fits in a small beaker.

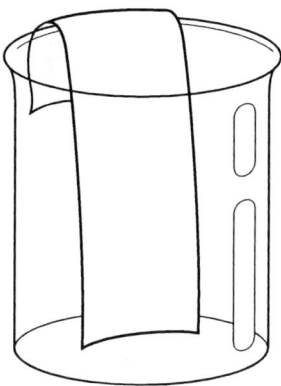

2  Pour 3 cm³ of propanone into a mortar.
3  Put some fresh grass leaves in the mortar and grind them up with the pestle.
4  Remove the filter paper from the beaker and pour propanone into the beaker to a depth of 1 cm.
5  Take a sample of propanone from the mortar with a dropping pipette or the end of a glass rod and put three drops in a line 2 cm from the lower edge of the paper.

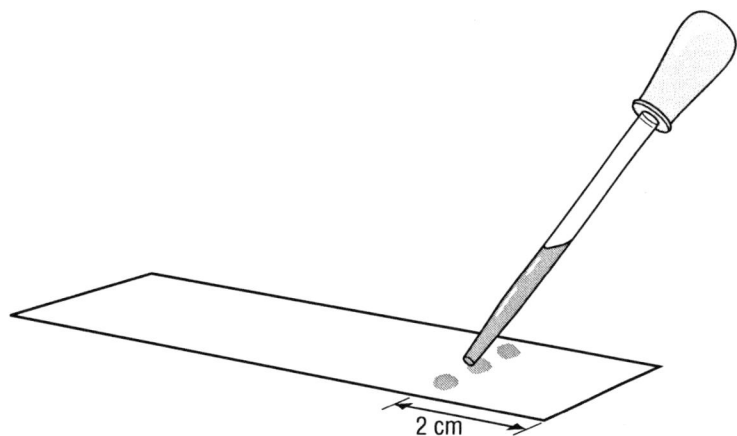

6  Place the filter paper in the propanone in the beaker and cover the beaker with a watch glass. Watch the propanone rise through the filter paper and look for the separation of different coloured substances.

## SEPARATION OF MIXTURES

# WORKSHEET 3.2  *End of chapter test*

1. Is there a fixed amount of each substance in **a)** a mixture, **b)** a compound?
2. Which of these statements about mixtures are true?
   - **i)** They are formed by chemical reactions.
   - **ii)** There is no change in heat energy when they are formed.
   - **iii)** The substances in the mixture retain their individual properties.
3. What is a suspension? Give an example.
4. What kind of mixture is smoke?
5. Milk is formed from water and fatty oil which is immiscible with water.
   - **a)** What does the word 'immiscible' tell you about the fatty oil?
   - **b)** Is milk **i)** an emulsion, **ii)** a suspension, or **iii)** a sediment?
6. Salt is stirred into cold water until no more will dissolve.
   - **a)** What can be done to the water to allow it to dissolve more salt?
   - **b)** Which is **i)** the solvent, **ii)** the solution, **iii)** the solute? Choose from these words:

   salt    water    mixture of salt and water

7. When would you use the following processes to separate solid and liquid mixtures:
   - **a)** decanting,
   - **b)** centrifuging?
   
   Explain how you would perform the separation in each case.
8. Why do substances separate on chromatography paper?
9. On this diagram of a Liebig condenser, draw arrows to show the path of **a)** the distillate, **b)** the cold water.

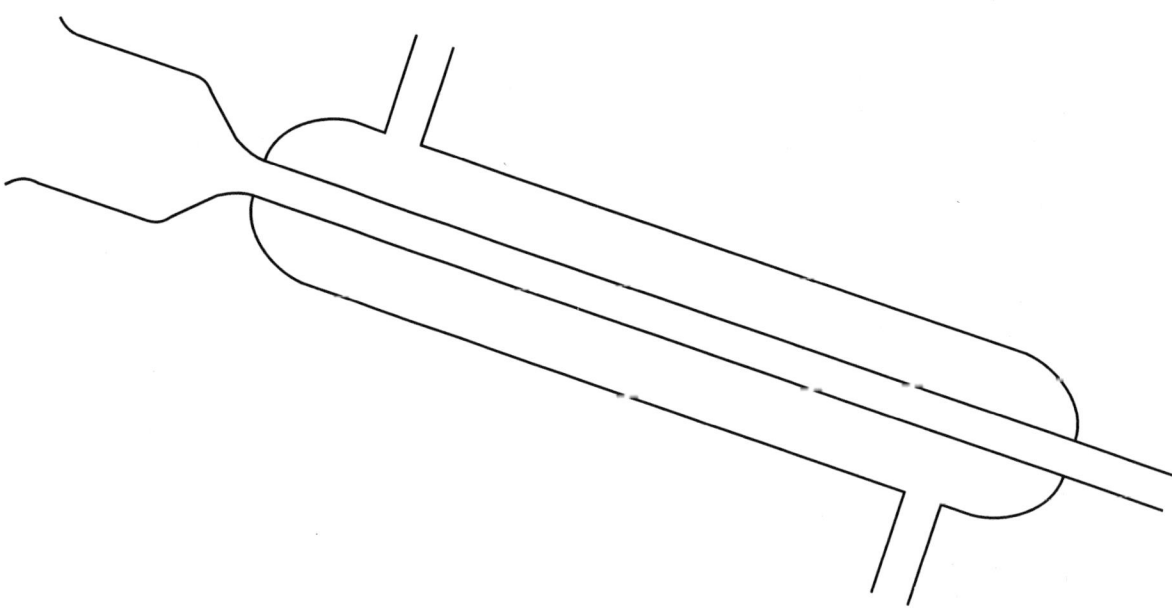

10. **a)** When a mixture of liquids with two different boiling points is heated, which liquid escapes first, **i)** the liquid with the higher boiling point, or **ii)** the liquid with the lower boiling point?
    **b)** What is the process called in which two liquids are separated by heating them?
11. **a)** What would you use a separating funnel for?
    **b)** How does it work?

# 4 Elements and atoms

## Answers

### Changing the idea of elements
(PB page 47)

1 Boyle believed elements could be found by trying to break down substances. If a substance could not be broken down it was an element.
2 Lavoisier weighed an amount of water and the pelican apparatus. He boiled the water for 101 days in the pelican then weighed them both again. He found that the weight of water remained unchanged and that the weight of the sediment was equal to the weight of the material lost by the pelican.
3 He weighed them (or found their mass).

### Discovery of the elements
(PB page 48)

1 a) 1   b) 19   c) 50
2 H. Davy, M.H. Klaproth, J.J. Berzelius
3 13 and G.C. de Hevesy (half Swedish)
4 H. Davy

### Dalton's atomic theory (PB page 52)

1 a) Substances are made up of atoms.
  b) Atoms cannot be destroyed.
2 Their atoms have different weights or masses.
3 J. Proust
4 We now know that atoms can be divided into smaller particles – they contain protons and electrons – and that atoms of the same element may have different masses (isotopes, PB page 54).

### Atoms (PB pages 53 and 54)

5 The statement is good in the following respects:

- The nucleus is at the centre of the atom and the Sun is at the centre of the Solar System.
- Electrons move around the nucleus and planets move around the Sun.

The statement is not good in the following respects:

- The electrons are arranged in groups at different distances from the nucleus while each planet is at a different distance from the Sun.
- The electron and the nucleus have different electrical charges, while the Sun and the planets do not have an overall positive or negative charge.

6 2, 8, 18, 32, 18, 4
7 Isotopes are atoms of an element which have different numbers of neutrons in their nuclei.

### The fourth state of matter (PB page 54)

1 Plasma only occurs at very high temperatures in stars or at very low pressures on the Earth. It is made from electrons and ions which have separated. (The pupils may say that in other states the particles are atoms, as ions may not be covered in detail at this level.)

### Chemical symbols (PB page 56)

8 Elements are identified by the first letter of their name but where two elements start with the same letter a second letter from one of the elements is used in its name.
9 Silver used to be called argentum and the letters from this name were used to identify silver. The potassium symbol comes from the word kalium which is another name for potassium. (Also, the symbol S is used for sulphur, and P for phosphorus.)
10 Some elements were named after their properties or after places or people.

### End of chapter question (PB page 56)

1 The model is not good in explaining the structure of the atom. It describes the overall spherical shape of the atom but does not show how the electrons are related to the nucleus.

### End of chapter test (WORKSHEET 4.2, TRB page 26)

1 which cannot be broken down into simpler substances
2 mercury and bromine
3 two or more elements combined together

# ELEMENTS AND ATOMS

4 No – the appearance of the compound is different, the melting point is over 700°C higher and the boiling point is over 600°C higher.

5

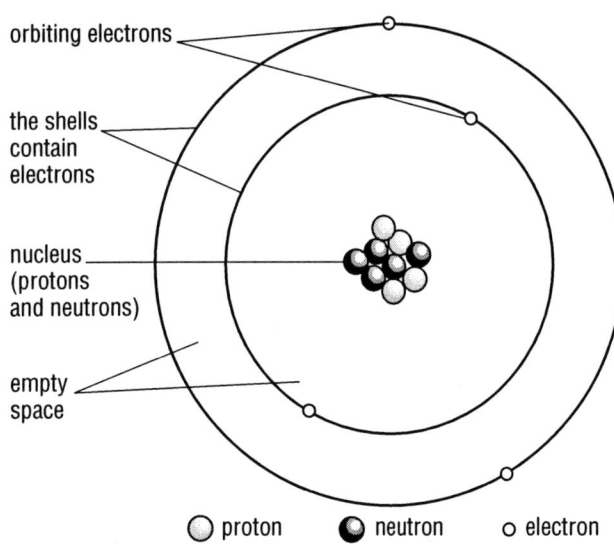

- orbiting electrons
- the shells contain electrons
- nucleus (protons and neutrons)
- empty space

○ proton   ◉ neutron   ○ electron

6 **a)** negative charge  **b)** positive charge
   **c)** no charge

7 Eight, because each proton has one positive electrical charge which balances the negative electrical charge carried by an electron. Eight protons are needed to balance the charges of the eight electrons to make the atom neutral.

8 isotopes

# IT input

Hall of Fame:

- Robert Boyle, PB page 47
- Antoine Lavoisier, PB page 47
- Hennig Brand, PB page 48
- Henry Cavendish, PB page 48
- Carl Scheele, PB page 48
- Jöns J. Berzelius, PB page 48
- William H. Wollaston, PB page 49
- Humphry Davy, PB page 49
- William Ramsay, PB page 50

CD-ROMs: there are several CD-ROMs that deal with the elements and periodic table. These vary in approach and usefulness, but the best of them are very good and are sure to enhance the pupils' interest and understanding. You should choose a title that is suitable for this age and ability level, and you should be familiar with its use.

# Activities

## Activity 4.1  Atomic modelling

*Atoms* (PB page 52)

Ask the pupils to make three-dimensional models of a hydrogen atom (one proton and one electron), a helium atom (two protons, two neutrons and two electrons) and a carbon atom (six protons, six neutrons and six electrons). They may choose materials such as cardboard, wire, Plasticine, marbles, glue and sticky paper from which to make their models. Ask the pupils to compare the three atoms; look for answers which show the relationship of two hydrogen atoms to one helium atom and three helium atoms to one carbon atom. Look also for the explanation that the electrons' positions cannot be located with certainty as they move very quickly.

**Preparation**
- Cardboard, wire or pipe cleaners, Plasticine, marbles, glue, sticky paper

**Safety**
- Eye protection must be worn when making models with wire.

## Activity 4.2  How big is a carbon atom?

*Atoms* (PB page 52)

WORKSHEET 4.1 How big is a carbon atom?
(TRB page 25)
This activity can be tried with older pupils. The aim is to show how the problem of atom size can be addressed rather than to find the exact size of an atom. Allow the pupils to measure several oil patches and conclude the activity by focusing on the order of size which the pupils are dealing with.

**Preparation**
- For each class group: tray, hand lens, wire loop, half-metre ruler
- Chemicals: talc or lycopodium powder, olive oil

**Safety**
- Lycopodium powder is a protein and theoretically could provoke an allergic reaction in some pupils. However, the chance is very small and has not been observed in the school situation. Try to avoid getting dust in the air.

ELEMENTS AND ATOMS

# WORKSHEET 4.1 *How big is a carbon atom?*

**✖** Lycopodium powder is an irritant – try to avoid getting the dust in the air

1. Fill a tray to the brim with water.
2. Cover the surface with a light coating of powder.
3. Use a wire loop, magnifying glass and ruler to make an oil drop 0.5 mm in diameter.
4. Dip the loop into the water at the centre of the tray.
5. Measure the diameter of the patch of oil.

    The volume of the oil drop $= \frac{4}{3} \pi$ (radius of drop)$^3$
    The area of the oil patch $= \pi$ (radius of patch)$^2$
    The thickness of the patch $=$ volume/area

6. The oil patch is only one oil molecule thick and the molecule is made up of 12 carbon atoms. How big is a carbon atom? Use the space below for your calculations.

ELEMENTS AND ATOMS

# WORKSHEET 4.2  *End of chapter test*

1  Complete this sentence:
   An element is a substance _____.
2  Which elements are liquid at room temperature?
3  Complete this sentence:
   A compound is made from _____.
4

| Substance | Appearance | Melting point in °C | Boiling point in °C |
|---|---|---|---|
| element | silver white surface | 98 | 804 |
| compound | white crystal | 801 | 1420 |

An element takes part in a chemical reaction to form a compound. Does it keep its properties when it forms the compound? Use the table to give reasons for your answer.

5  Draw and label the parts of an atom.
6  What is the electrical charge on **a)** an electron, **b)** a proton, **c)** a neutron?
7  An electrically neutral atom has eight electrons. How many protons has it got? Explain your answer.
8  Complete this sentence:
   Atoms of the same element which have different numbers of neutrons are called _____.

---

# WORKSHEET 4.2  *End of chapter test*

1  Complete this sentence:
   An element is a substance _____.
2  Which elements are liquid at room temperature?
3  Complete this sentence:
   A compound is made from _____.
4

| Substance | Appearance | Melting point in °C | Boiling point in °C |
|---|---|---|---|
| element | silver white surface | 98 | 804 |
| compound | white crystal | 801 | 1420 |

An element takes part in a chemical reaction to form a compound. Does it keep its properties when it forms the compound? Use the table to give reasons for your answer.

5  Draw and label the parts of an atom.
6  What is the electrical charge on **a)** an electron, **b)** a proton, **c)** a neutron?
7  An electrically neutral atom has eight electrons. How many protons has it got? Explain your answer.
8  Complete this sentence:
   Atoms of the same element which have different numbers of neutrons are called _____.

# 5 Chemical reactions

## Answers

### Reactants and products (PB page 57)

1. A product is a substance that forms as a result of a chemical reaction, a reactant is a substance that takes part in a chemical reaction.
2. If the reaction is reversible it will have arrows pointing in both directions (⇌). If the reaction is not reversible the arrow will point in only one direction.

### Chemical reactions and energy (PB page 58)

3. Energy may be taken in or given out.
4. The flame from the match provides enough energy for the wax in the wick to start to burn, then more energy is released by the burning wax.

### Types of chemical reaction (PB pages 60—62)

5. The production of lime would be reduced. Carbon dioxide produced by heating the limestone would combine with the calcium oxide and form calcium carbonate again.
6. a) The products calcium oxide and carbon dioxide react together to form calcium carbonate.
   b) calcium carbonate ⇌ calcium oxide + carbon dioxide
7. calcium oxide + water → calcium hydroxide
8. A substance breaks down to form two or more products.
9. hydrated cobalt chloride → anhydrous cobalt chloride + water

### Synthesis (PB page 64)

10. In a synthesis reaction two or more substances join together to make a compound. In a decomposition reaction a compound breaks down to form two or more substances.

### Reduction (PB page 65)

11. In an oxidation reaction oxygen is added to a substance or hydrogen is removed from it. In a reduction reaction oxygen is taken from a substance or hydrogen is added to it.
12. When the reactants react together reactant A may give oxygen or hydrogen to reactant B while reactant B receives oxygen or hydrogen from reactant A.

### Speed of chemical reactions (PB page 67)

13. The milk by the radiator will have turned sour while the milk in the fridge has not. The heat will have speeded up the chemical reactions which make the milk sour. The sourness is caused by living organisms that feed and respire in the milk. Raising the temperature speeds up these reactions.
14. The reaction will be weaker because the concentration of the vinegar has been reduced.
15. a) 24 cm$^2$   b) 48 cm$^2$
    c) The surface area is larger.
16. More of the stain had been removed from the cloth in the bowl with the washing powder. The enzymes in the biological washing powder are catalysts and have speeded up the reaction which removes the blood from the cloth.

### End of chapter questions (PB page 68)

1. sulphuric acid + sodium hydroxide → sodium sulphate + water
   It is a neutralisation reaction.
2. In both a decomposition reaction and fermentation a compound is broken down into simpler compounds. However, a decomposition reaction takes place without the involvement of a living organism while in a fermentation reaction the living organism called yeast is required. So in one way the reactions are alike but in another way they are not.

## CHEMICAL REACTIONS

## End of chapter test (WORKSHEET 5.6, TRB page 36)

1. **a) i)** carbon dioxide and water
   **ii)** methane and oxygen
   **b)** an oxidation reaction
2. $\rightleftharpoons$
3. a synthesis reaction
4. **a)** magnesium and oxygen
   **b)** magnesium oxide
   **c)** Energy is given out.
   **d)** Oxygen has combined with the magnesium, and the extra weight is due to the oxygen in the compound.
5. Light causes the silver chloride to decompose into silver and chlorine.
6. hydrogen and oxygen
7. Bubble the gas through a test-tube of lime water. The lime water would change from a clear colourless solution to a liquid containing a white precipitate.
8. Anhydrous copper sulphate changes from white to blue in the presence of water; anhydrous cobalt chloride changes from blue to pink.
9. **a)** calcium and oxygen
   **b)** It swells up and becomes hot and forms calcium hydroxide.
   **c)** Slaked lime, which is used as mortar to hold bricks together.
10. a neutralisation reaction
11. a reduction reaction
12. a fermentation reaction
13. The reaction would slow down. Temperature affects the speed of a reaction. The higher the temperature the faster the reaction takes place. In this case the temperature is lowered so the reaction would slow down.
14. Tube 2, because the powdered solid offers a larger surface area to the acid and the more concentrated acid has more 'particles' (ions) which can take part in the reaction.
15. Catalysts speed up chemical reactions in industry so products can be made faster. They slow down the deterioration of processed foods so that they remain edible longer and can be stored longer. Enzymes are catalysts which control reactions in the body.

## IT input

Pupils can use CD-ROMs and the Internet to search for information on limestone.

## Activities

### Activity 5.1 Oxidation of magnesium

*Magnesium oxide* (PB page 64) and *Rise and fall of the phlogiston theory* (PB page 86)

WORKSHEET 5.1 Oxidation of magnesium (TRB page 31)

Although the activity is presented here in the context of oxidation, it can also be used to support the work on the phlogiston theory in Chapter 7 and be set as an investigation.

Oxidation of a metal by air leads to a change in mass. The pupils can record the mass of a substance before and after oxidation. They will realise that an increase in mass has occurred. This is a useful experiment both to show oxidation by air and to encourage the pupils to realise that a chemical change in the composition of the substance has occurred. This experiment may be performed as a determination of the empirical formula of magnesium oxide. The pupils will develop their practical and organisational skills.

Demonstrate the use of the crucible, tongs and pipe-clay triangle before introducing the practical on Worksheet 5.1.

If the activity is set as an investigation it can be extended by asking the pupils to predict what the mass of the products would be if **a)** a smaller amount and **b)** a larger amount of magnesium was used and then allowing them to test their prediction. The groups should compare their results and assess the factors, such as differences in equipment or in experimental competence, that may contribute to variations in the results of the whole class.

### Preparation
- For each class group: Bunsen burner, heatproof mat, tripod, pipe-clay triangle, tongs, crucible and crucible lid, emery paper
- Chemicals: magnesium ribbon
- Top pan balance

# ACTIVITIES

**Safety**

- Eye protection must be worn.
- Magnesium may cause damage to the eyes. Do not look directly at burning magnesium.
- Make sure that the tripods have cooled down before clearing them away.

## Activity 5.2 Oxidation of zinc by sulphuric acid

### Oxidation (PB page 64)

WORKSHEET 5.2 Oxidation of zinc by sulphuric acid (TRB page 32)

Oxidation may be thought of as the loss of hydrogen. This experiment allows the pupils to observe this loss of gas and to test the gas for hydrogen. They are developing practical skills and observational skills as well as gaining information on types of chemical reactions. Alternatively, the oxidation may be done as a teacher demonstration.

**Preparation**

- For each class group: Buchner flask, bungs, rubber tubing and delivery tube, water bath, test-tubes, splints
- Chemicals: zinc granules, 1.0 M sulphuric acid

**Safety**

- Eye protection must be worn.
- Hydrogen/air mixture is explosive: do not allow pupils to ignite hydrogen at the delivery tubes.
- Dilute sulphuric acid is irritating to the eyes and skin and may cause burns.

## Activity 5.3 Displacement reactions of metals

### Displacement (PB page 65)

WORKSHEET 5.3 Displacement reactions (TRB page 33)

The worksheet provides a series of small test-tube experiments that pupils may perform. It studies the displacement reactions of a series of metals and from these pupils can construct a reactivity series. The pupils will develop practical skills and organisational skills since it is essential to present the data in a clear concise format. They will study the different reactivities of metals and this will enable them to understand better how all metals are different.

**Preparation**

**Procedure 1** Displacement of metals from solution

- For each class group: test-tubes
- Chemicals: 0.5 M solutions of copper sulphate, magnesium sulphate and iron sulphate, strips of copper, magnesium and iron

**Procedure 2** Reaction of metals with an acid

- For each class group: test-tubes, bung with delivery tube, 250 cm$^3$ graduated syringe, stop clock
- Chemicals: strips of tin, copper, iron, zinc and magnesium, 1.0 M hydrochloric acid

**Safety**

- Eye protection must be worn.
- Remind pupils to be careful when handling chemicals.

## Activity 5.4 Investigating precipitation reactions

### Precipitation (PB page 66)

WORKSHEET 5.4 Precipitation reactions (TRB page 34)

This is an investigation into identifying common ions by their precipitation reactions. The pupils are provided with information on the reactions of ions in solution and the precipitates they form. From this information the pupils are required to identify the bottles of reagents that have lost their labels.

**Preparation**

- For each class group: test-tubes, dropping pipette
- Chemicals: 1.0 M calcium chloride, 1.0 M hydrochloric acid, 0.5 M iron(II) sulphate, 0.5 M iron(II) chloride, 1.0 M aluminium sulphate, 0.05 M silver nitrate, 0.1 M barium chloride, 1.0 M sodium hydroxide

**Safety**

- Eye protection must be worn.
- Silver nitrate is irritating to the eyes and skin, may cause blackening of skin or burns, and is harmful by ingestion.
- Barium chloride is harmful and may cause nausea, stomach pain and vomiting if swallowed and is irritating to the eyes.
- Sodium hydroxide is corrosive, irritant and harmful as a spray.

# CHEMICAL REACTIONS

## Activity 5.5 Investigating the speed of a reaction

### Speed of chemical reactions
(PB page 67)

WORKSHEET 5.5 The speed of a reaction
(TRB page 35)

This is a familiar exercise for laboratory investigations and pupils can use the investigation sheets to develop their ideas. By carrying out the practical work the pupils will develop skills with apparatus. Several reactions may be studied but the easiest is the reaction between calcium carbonate and hydrochloric acid. It enables the pupils to monitor the evolution of carbon dioxide and thus appreciate the difference in speed on changing conditions.

When checking the pupils' plans, discuss safety issues and remind them that more concentrated hydrochloric acid is an irritant.

**Preparation**
- For each class group: dropping funnel, Buchner flask, tubing, graduated syringe
- Chemicals: calcium carbonate as a powder, marble chips and solid cubes, 1.0 M hydrochloric acid

**Safety**
- Eye protection must be worn.
- Remind pupils to be careful when handling chemicals.

## Activity 5.6 Catalytic decomposition of hydrogen peroxide

### Catalyst (PB page 67)

This practical is a teacher demonstration to show how a decomposition reaction can be speeded up by the use of a catalyst. Hydrogen peroxide decomposes slowly to produce water and oxygen. This reaction can be speeded up by adding a manganese(IV) oxide catalyst. The best way of demonstrating this experiment is to set up five 100 cm$^3$ conical flasks containing 100, 80, 60, 40 and 20 volume hydrogen peroxide solution. It will be evident that volumes of oxygen are not being produced before adding the catalyst. Add a small amount of manganese(IV) oxide to the 20 volume hydrogen peroxide solution and oxygen will be evolved, showing the decomposition reaction. Repeat the experiment with the higher volume solutions and there will be an increase in the rate of oxygen evolution. This shows both the action of a catalyst and the effect of a change in concentration of the hydrogen peroxide.

**Preparation**
- For the teacher: beakers or conical flasks
- Chemicals: manganese(IV) oxide, 100, 80, 60, 40 and 20 volume hydrogen peroxide solutions prepared by dilution as follows:

    80 volume = 16 cm$^3$ 100% +  4 cm$^3$ water
    60 volume = 12 cm$^3$ 100% +  8 cm$^3$ water
    40 volume =  8 cm$^3$ 100% + 12 cm$^3$ water
    20 volume =  4 cm$^3$ 100% + 16 cm$^3$ water

**Safety**
- Eye protection must be worn.
- Hydrogen peroxide causes severe burns and is irritating to the respiratory system.
- Manganese(IV) oxide is harmful by ingestion.

# WORKSHEET 5.1 *Oxidation of magnesium*

- Eye protection must be worn
- ! Do not look directly at burning magnesium
- ! Make sure that the tripod has cooled down before clearing it away

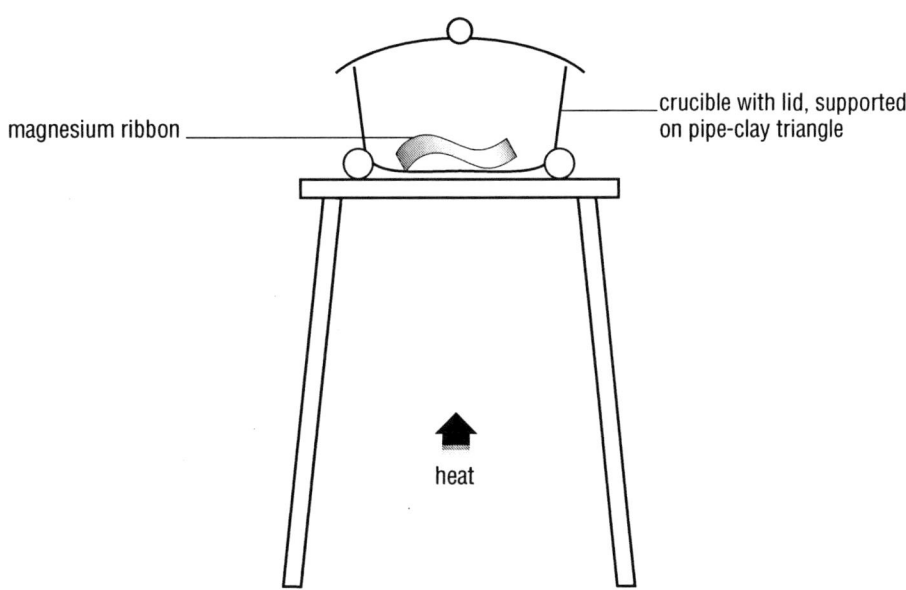

1. Clean a small strip of magnesium ribbon with emery paper.
2. Record the mass of a crucible and lid on a balance (mass A1).
3. Place the magnesium ribbon in the crucible, replace the lid and record this mass (mass A2).
4. Place the crucible on the pipe-clay triangle and heat strongly.
5. Re-weigh the crucible and lid (mass A3).
6. Record these results in a suitable table below.
7. How has the weight changed? Can you explain these results?

**CHEMICAL REACTIONS**

# WORKSHEET 5.2 *Oxidation of zinc by sulphuric acid*

 Eye protection must be worn

 Handle sulphuric acid with great care

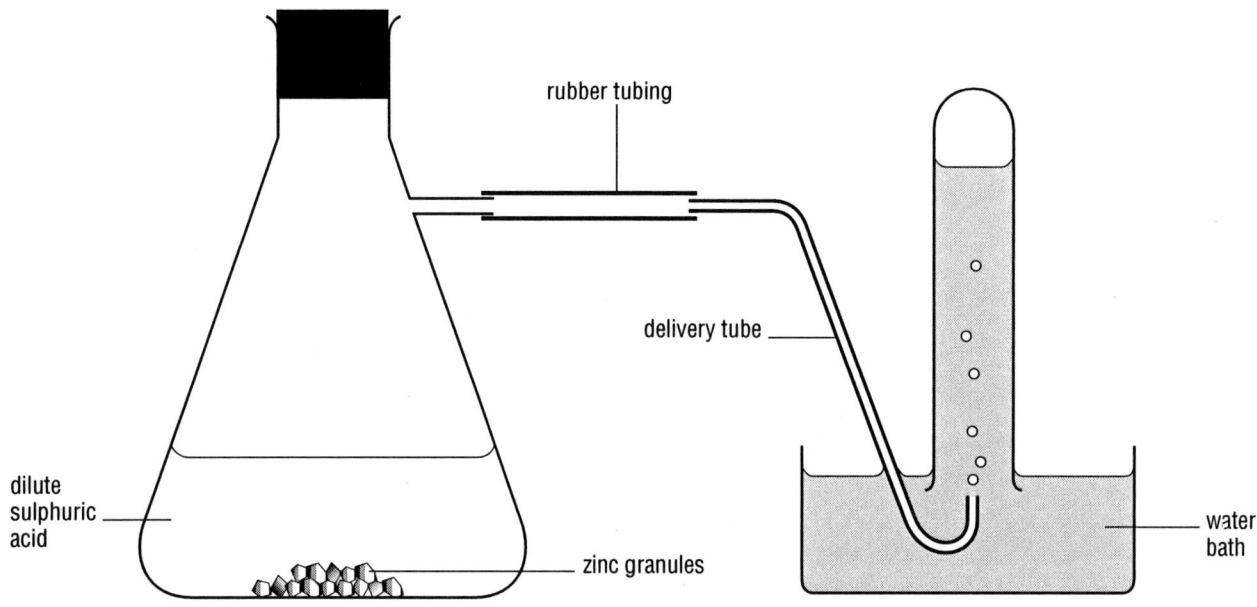

1. Set up the apparatus by attaching the rubber tubing to the side arm of the Buchner flask. Attach the delivery tube to the other end of the rubber tubing. Place the delivery tube in a water bath and immerse the end of the tube.
2. Place some sulphuric acid into the Buchner flask and add a small amount of zinc. Immediately place the bung on the Buchner flask and place a test-tube full of water over the end of the delivery tube. Collect test-tubes full of gas and stopper them under the water to prevent any gas escaping. The first test-tube may have to be discarded because it will contain mostly air.
3. Test the gas produced for hydrogen by placing a lighted splint in the opening of the test-tube. If the gas is hydrogen, a squeaky pop will be heard.

# WORKSHEET 5.3 *Displacement reactions*

 Eye protection must be worn

Handle all chemicals with great care

**Procedure 1: Displacement of metals from solution**
1. Set up three test-tubes, each containing a different solution. They should be different colours.
2. Place a piece of copper metal in each of the test-tubes. List your observations.
3. Set up three fresh test-tubes as in step 1.
4. Repeat step 2 with a piece of iron.
5. Repeat step 2 with a piece of magnesium.
6. From your table of results, decide which metals are the most and the least reactive.

**Procedure 2: Reaction of metals with an acid**
1. In a test-tube place a small amount, about 2 $cm^3$, of hydrochloric acid.
2. Attach a rubber bung with a delivery tube to the test-tube and place a syringe on the end of this tube.
3. Place a piece of tin in the acid and time how long it takes for the syringe to reach a certain volume.
4. Repeat with the other metals.
5. Place the metals in order of increasing reactivity depending upon how quickly they react with the acid.

Use the space below to construct tables of your results.

## CHEMICAL REACTIONS

# WORKSHEET 5.4 *Precipitation reactions*

 Eye protection must be worn

 Handle the solutions of barium chloride, silver nitrate and sodium hydroxide with great care

Five solutions A–E have been prepared by the technician; unfortunately they have lost their labels and she needs help in identifying the bottles. She has made up the following solutions:

- hydrochloric acid
- iron sulphate
- aluminium sulphate
- iron chloride
- calcium chloride

You are provided with the following data:

- test for sulphate – barium chloride solution gives a white precipitate
- test for chloride – silver nitrate solution gives a white precipitate
- test for iron – sodium hydroxide solution gives a green precipitate which may turn brown
- test for calcium – sodium hydroxide solution gives a white precipitate
- test for aluminium – sodium hydroxide solution gives a white precipitate

Use the space below to design a safe experiment and, when checked by your teacher, carry it out to identify the reagents A–E.

# WORKSHEET 5.5 *The speed of a reaction*

 Eye protection must be worn

! Handle the chemicals with great care

Investigate how the speed of a reaction changes when the conditions are altered.

The conditions you may change are:

- temperature
- concentration of acid
- particle size

Use the space below to design your experiments. Have your teacher check your plans before you proceed with experimenting.

# CHEMICAL REACTIONS

## WORKSHEET 5.6 *End of chapter test*

1. In the reaction

    methane + oxygen → carbon dioxide + water

    a) which chemicals are **i)** the products, **ii)** the reactants?
    b) Is it **i)** a decomposition reaction, **ii)** a precipitation reaction, or **iii)** an oxidation reaction?

2. What symbol is used to show that a reaction is reversible?

3. Is the reaction

    nitrogen + hydrogen → ammonia

    **i)** a synthesis reaction, **ii)** a decomposition reaction, or **iii)** a precipitation reaction?

4. When a piece of magnesium is heated and then plunged into oxygen, a brilliant white light is produced and a white powder forms.
    a) What are the reactants in this reaction?
    b) What is the product of the reaction?
    c) Is energy given out or taken in when the reaction is taking place?
    d) The powder weighs more than the original piece of magnesium. Why is this?

5. How does light affect silver chloride?

6. What elements are produced when a current of electricity is passed through water?

7. Describe how you would test a gas to see if it was carbon dioxide. What change would you expect to see if the gas was carbon dioxide?

8. Name two chemicals that you could use to test for the presence of water. For each one describe the change that takes place when water is present.

9. a) What are the elements present in lime?
    b) What happens to lime when water is added to it?
    c) What is the common name for this substance and how is it used in the building industry?

10. What kind of reaction occurs between an acid and a base?

11. What kind of reaction takes place when a substance has oxygen removed from it or hydrogen added to it?

12. What kind of chemical reaction takes place using yeast?

13. A liquid in which a chemical reaction was taking place is cooled down. How would this affect the reaction? Explain your answer.

14. A lump of solid material was put into a dilute acid in test-tube 1 and the same mass of powdered solid was put in a more concentrated acid in test-tube 2. In which tube would the faster reaction occur? Explain your answer.

15. Why are catalysts useful substances?

# 6 Acids and bases

## Answers

### The acid in vinegar (PB page 70)

1 Oxygen from the air dissolves in the wine and reacts with the ethanol to form ethanoic acid, which makes the wine turn sour.

### Organic acids and mineral acids
(PB page 70)

2 a) Organic acids came from living organisms – plants and animals.
  b) Mineral acids came from materials in rocks.
3 a) The upper acids are dilute as dil. = dilute, and lower ones are concentrated as conc. = concentrated.
  b) A dilute solution contains more solvent (e.g. water) than a concentrated solution.

### Acids and metals (PB page 71)

4 a) The hydrogen pushes out of the flask and delivery tube into the test-tube.
  b) The level of the water in the test-tube goes down.
5 magnesium + sulphuric acid
   → magnesium sulphate + hydrogen

### Acids and carbonates (PB page 71)

6 copper carbonate + sulphuric acid
   → copper sulphate + water + carbon dioxide

### Bases (PB page 72)

7 sodium hydroxide, calcium carbonate, copper oxide, sodium hydrogencarbonate

### Detecting acids and alkalis
(PB page 73)

8 When a base is added to an acid it cancels out the acid's properties and a product with neutral properties is produced. An alkali, which is a soluble base, will turn red litmus blue while an acid will turn blue litmus red. The pH values of acids are from 1 to 6 while the pH values of alkalis are from 8 to 14.
9 They are both corrosive and can be detected by the use of litmus or universal indicator.

### Strong and weak acids and alkalis
(PB pages 73 and 74)

10 a) i) A, C, D  ii) B, E, F
   b) A red, B purple, C yellow, D pink, E purple, F light blue
   c) The pH would become lower as the sourness is due to the development of acids.
11 sulphuric acid, car battery acid, washing-up liquid, milk of magnesia, metal polish, oven cleaner
12 strong acids: **A**, **D**, sulphuric acid, battery acid; weak acids: **C**, washing-up liquid; strong alkalis: **E**, **B**, oven cleaner; weak alkalis: **F**, milk of magnesia, metal polish
13 It is a strong acid, because it dissolved silver and because it is a mineral acid like sulphuric acid.
14 pH about 6 – a weak acid

### Neutralisation (PB page 74)

15 a) sulphuric acid + zinc oxide
      → zinc sulphate + water
   b) hydrochloric acid + calcium hydroxide
      → calcium chloride + water
   c) nitric acid + calcium carbonate
      → calcium nitrate + water + carbon dioxide
16 Carbon dioxide is produced.

### End of chapter questions (PB page 76)

1 This may include vinegar, sour milk, acid giving taste to fruits, the acids which make stings, the acid in our stomach, acid produced in exercise which gives pain, uric acid (an excretory product), acid used in car batteries. Using other parts of the book may lead to mention of acids in the manufacture of products we use and the danger of acid rain.
2 The pH of the products is 7. If universal indicator is used it turns green to show a pH of 7; if a pH meter is used the pH is displayed.

### End of chapter test (WORKSHEET 6.7, TRB page 46)

1 a) citric acid, methanoic acid, tartaric acid
  b) hydrochloric acid, sulphuric acid, nitric acid

# ACIDS AND BASES

2 **a)** hydrogen and the metal salt
**b)** carbon dioxide, the metal salt and water
3 oxides, hydroxides and carbonates
4 hydrogencarbonates
5 a base that is soluble in water, e.g. sodium hydroxide, potassium hydroxide
6 Red litmus paper is used to test for alkalis: if an alkali is present it turns blue. Blue litmus paper is used to test for acids: if an acid is present it turns red.
7 **a)** 0 **b)** 6 **c)** 14 **d)** 8
8 **a)** 7 **b)** neutral
9 A bee sting is acidic and soap is an alkali so the acid is neutralised. A wasp sting is alkaline and vinegar is an acid which can neutralise it.
10 **a)** hydrochloric acid, water
**b)** zinc, hydrogen
**c) a)** neutralisation **b)** displacement

## IT input

Pupils can use CD-ROMs and the Internet to search for information on sulphuric acid and sodium hydroxide.

## Activities

### Activity 6.1 The pH of a range of acids and alkalis

*Strong and weak acids and alkalis* (PB page 73)

WORKSHEET 6.1 Acids and alkalis (TRB page 40)
This activity is best done once the pupils have been introduced to the pH scale of acids and bases. They will be able to appreciate the difference between strong and weak acids and bases and dilute and concentrated solutions. A range of common acids and alkalis are set up and the pH tested using universal indicator solution. Pupils will develop a greater understanding of the difference between acids and alkalis and the varying pH values of strong and weak solutions.

**Preparation**
- For each class group: test-tubes
- Chemicals: 1 M hydrochloric acid, 1 M sodium hydroxide, 1 M ethanoic acid, 1 M ammonium hydroxide, lemon juice, sodium bicarbonate, milk, water, toothpaste, lime water, universal indicator solution

**Safety**
- Eye protection must be worn.
- Sodium hydroxide solution is corrosive.

### Activity 6.2 Bases and alkalis

*Bases* (PB page 71)

WORKSHEET 6.2 Bases and alkalis (TRB page 41)
Once the pupils are familiar with pH as a means of measuring the acidity or alkalinity of a solution, they may be introduced to the idea of bases and alkalis. This is often quite difficult for pupils to understand. If a metal oxide is soluble in water it produces an alkaline solution. The pupils again use universal indicator solution to test whether the solid has produced an alkaline solution when put into water.

**Preparation**
- For each class group: test-tubes
- Chemicals: sodium carbonate, calcium carbonate, magnesium oxide, tin oxide, iron oxide, sodium hydrogencarbonate, potassium hydrogencarbonate, calcium hydroxide, universal indicator solution

**Safety**
- Eye protection must be worn.

### Activity 6.3 Neutralisation reactions

*Neutralisation* (PB page 74)

WORKSHEET 6.3 Neutralisation (TRB page 42)
Once the pupils are familiar and secure about acids and bases and their different pH values, the idea of neutralisation may be introduced. They will have studied neutralisation reactions and be aware that when an acid is added to an alkali the pH changes to neutral. If too much acid is added the pH will become lower, showing an excess of acid.

**Preparation**
- For each class group: boiling tubes, measuring cylinders
- Chemicals: 0.5 M solutions of sodium hydroxide, hydrochloric acid, ammonium hydroxide and ethanoic acid, universal indicator solution

**Safety**
- Eye protection must be worn.
- Sodium hydroxide solution is corrosive.

# ACTIVITIES

## Activity 6.4 Formation of salts

### Neutralisation (PB page 74)

WORKSHEET 6.4 Salt formation (TRB page 43)
After discovering the reactions of acids and alkalis the pupils may prepare a salt by neutralisation. Almost any metal salt can be prepared by reaction with an acid, followed by crystallisation. The procedure on the worksheet will enable pupils to perform a neutralisation reaction and isolate the salt, gaining increased practical skills.

### Preparation
- For each class group: beakers, filter funnel and paper, Bunsen burner, heatproof mat, tripod, gauze
- Chemicals: metal oxides or carbonates, e.g. copper carbonate, magnesium oxide, iron carbonate; dilute acid solutions depending on the salt wanted, e.g. 0.5 M sulphuric acid, 0.5 M hydrochloric acid, ice

### Safety
- Eye protection must be worn.
- Sulphuric acid is an irritant.
- Make sure that the tripods have cooled down before clearing them away.

## Activity 6.5 Reaction of acids and metals

### Acids and metals (PB page 70)

WORKSHEET 6.5 Acids and metals (TRB page 44)
This practical is used to show how metals dissolve in acid to produce a salt with the evolution of hydrogen. It may be performed as in Activity 5.3 (procedure 2) or it may be done to show the production of a salt, as in Activity 6.4. The gas may be collected under water via a delivery tube to another tube and the gas tested for hydrogen (by producing a squeaky pop with a lighted splint).

### Preparation
- For each class group: conical flask, two-holed bung with delivery tube attached, dropping funnel, water bath, test-tubes, splints
- Chemicals: magnesium, calcium, iron, zinc, 1.0 M hydrochloric acid

### Safety
- Eye protection must be worn.
- Do not allow pupils to light hydrogen as it comes out of the delivery tube.

## Activity 6.6 Reaction of metal carbonates and acids

### Acids and carbonates (PB page 71)

WORKSHEET 6.6 Acids and carbonates (TRB page 45)
This practical may have been studied as an investigation into the speed of a reaction (Activity 5.5).

The practical skills required are the same as for Activity 6.5 and it may be performed alongside it. The same apparatus is used and the gas is collected in the same manner. This time, however, the gas is carbon dioxide and is heavier than air. The test for this gas is that it produces a cloudy precipitate when passed through lime water.

### Preparation
- For each class group: dropping funnel, Buchner flask, rubber tubing, graduated syringe
- Chemicals: calcium carbonate as a powder, marble chips and solid cubes, hydrochloric acid (0.25, 0.5, 1.0 and 2.0 M), lime water

### Safety
- Eye protection must be worn.
- 2 M hydrochloric acid is an irritant.

ACIDS AND BASES

# WORKSHEET 6.1   *Acids and alkalis*

 Eye protection must be worn

 Handle all solutions with great care

1. Collect test-tubes and place a small amount of the different solutions in separate tubes. (If it is not a solution, dissolve the solid in a small amount of water to produce a solution.)
2. Label the test-tubes to ensure you know which solution is present in each tube.
3. Add a few drops of universal indicator solution to each tube and note the pH.
4. List the solutions in order of increasing pH in the space below.

ACIDS AND BASES

# WORKSHEET 6.2   *Bases and alkalis*

 Eye protection must be worn

1   Collect test-tubes. In the bottom of each tube place about 2 cm³ of water.
2   Place a small amount of a solid metal salt into the bottom of the tube and shake to dissolve it.
3   Once the solid has dissolved, add a few drops of universal indicator solution to the tube and shake gently. Record the pH. (Alternatively, dampen a piece of red litmus paper and dip it into the solution. If it turns blue the solution is alkaline.)
4   Set out your results in a table below.

■ ACIDS AND BASES

# WORKSHEET 6.3   *Neutralisation*

  Eye protection must be worn

Handle all solutions with great care

**Procedure**
Carry out the following steps using **a)** dilute hydrochloric acid and dilute sodium hydroxide, **b)** dilute ethanoic acid and dilute sodium hydroxide, **c)** dilute hydrochloric acid and dilute ammonium hydroxide.

1. Place 10 cm$^3$ of the dilute acid in a boiling tube and add a few drops of indicator solution.
2. Add 5 cm$^3$ of the dilute alkali and notice if there is any change in colour.
3. Add another 5 cm$^3$ of the alkali solution and note the change in colour.
4. Add a further 5 cm$^3$ of the alkali solution and note the colour.

**Questions**

1. What was the original colour of the universal indicator in the acid solution?

2. What information did this give about the pH of the solution?

3. Did any colour change occur when 5 cm$^3$ of the alkali solution was added? Why not?

4. How did the colour change after another 5 cm$^3$ of alkali solution was added?

5. What colour did the solution become as more alkali solution was added? Why?

# WORKSHEET 6.4 *Salt formation*

 Eye protection must be worn

 Handle acids with great care

 Make sure that the tripod has cooled down before clearing it away

1. Place 50 $cm^3$ of dilute acid into a beaker.
2. Slowly, little by little, add the solid metal compound. Be aware of any vigorous reaction.
3. Once all the compound has dissolved in the acid, filter the solution carefully through a filter paper in a filter funnel.
4. Evaporate off some of the solvent by heating over a Bunsen burner. Take care – do not have a roaring flame and do not allow the solution to spit.
5. Once the amount of solution has been reduced, allow it to cool to room temperature and then in ice. Crystals of the salt should start to form in the solution. If they do not, allow the solution to stand, covered, at room temperature overnight.

---

# WORKSHEET 6.4 *Salt formation*

 Eye protection must be worn

 Handle acids with great care

 Make sure that the tripod has cooled down before clearing it away

1. Place 50 $cm^3$ of dilute acid into a beaker.
2. Slowly, little by little, add the solid metal compound. Be aware of any vigorous reaction.
3. Once all the compound has dissolved in the acid, filter the solution carefully through a filter paper in a filter funnel.
4. Evaporate off some of the solvent by heating over a Bunsen burner. Take care – do not have a roaring flame and do not allow the solution to spit.
5. Once the amount of solution has been reduced, allow it to cool to room temperature and then in ice. Crystals of the salt should start to form in the solution. If they do not, allow the solution to stand, covered, at room temperature overnight.

# ACIDS AND BASES

# WORKSHEET 6.5   *Acids and metals*

 Eye protection must be worn

! Handle acids with great care

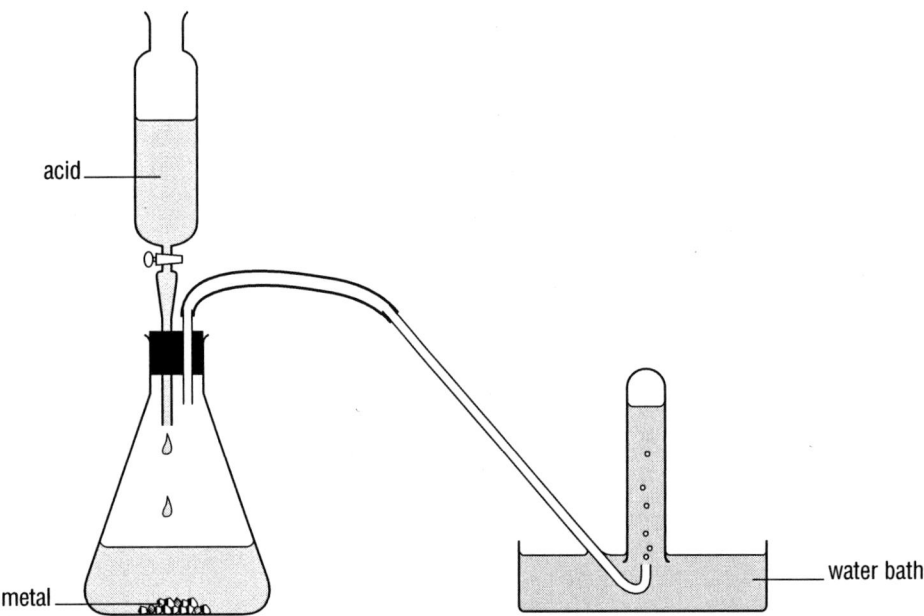

1. Collect a conical flask, a bung with delivery tube, a dropping funnel, a water bath and test-tubes.
2. Place the metal in the conical flask and stopper with the bung. Attach the dropping funnel to the bung.
3. Add the acid to the dropping funnel and immerse the delivery tube under water to collect the gas produced in an inverted test-tube filled with water.
4. Slowly add the acid to the metal in the conical flask by carefully opening the tap of the dropping funnel very slightly – you must produce a slow, steady flow of acid onto the metal.
5. Collect any gas produced in the test-tube and test for hydrogen by placing a lighted splint into the test-tube. If the gas is hydrogen it should produce a squeaky pop as it burns.

# WORKSHEET 6.6  *Acids and carbonates*

 Eye protection must be worn

 Handle hydrochloric acid with great care

1 Collect a Buchner flask, dropping funnel and bung, rubber tubing and graduated syringe.
2 Assemble the apparatus as shown below.

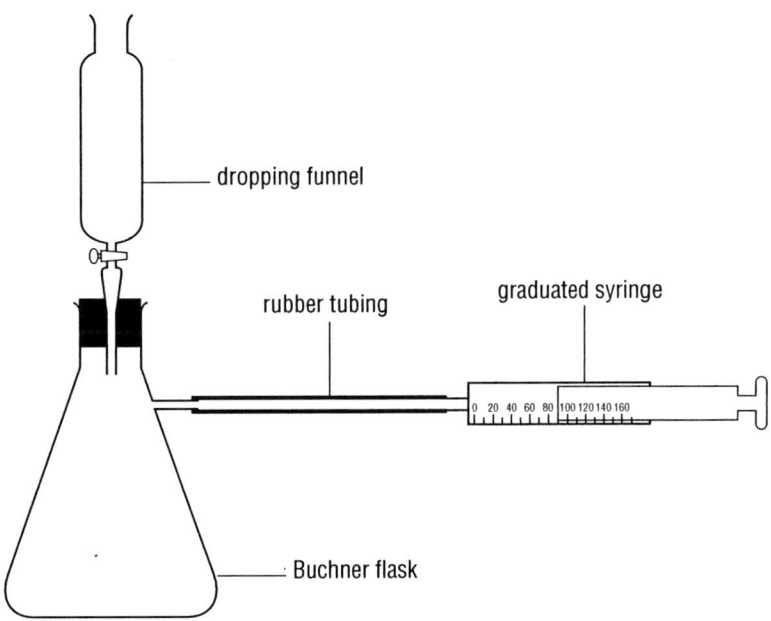

3 Weigh out a large piece of calcium carbonate.
4 Place the carbonate in the Buchner flask.
5 Pour 25 cm³ of 1.0 M hydrochloric acid into the dropping funnel.
6 Add 20 cm³ of the acid to the Buchner flask.
7 Record the time taken for 100 cm³ of carbon dioxide to be collected in the syringe.
8 Repeat the experiment using 0.25 M, 0.5 M and 2.0 M hydrochloric acid. Record your results in a table.
9 Repeat the experiment using different sized pieces of calcium carbonate. Record your results in a table.
10 What can you conclude from your results?

ACIDS AND BASES

# WORKSHEET 6.7  *End of chapter test*

1. Which of the following are **a)** organic acids, **b)** mineral acids?

    hydrochloric acid   citric acid   methanoic acid
    sulphuric acid   tartaric acid   nitric acid

2. What are the products when an acid reacts with **a)** a metal, **b)** a carbonate?
3. Which of the following metal compounds are bases?

    chlorides   oxides   hydroxides   sulphates   nitrates   carbonates

4. Name one other type of metal compound which is a base that is not featured in question 3.
5. What is an alkali? Give an example of a common alkali used in the laboratory.
6. How would you use litmus paper to identify an acid and an alkali?
7. Estimate the pH of **a)** a very strong acid, **b)** a very weak acid, **c)** a very strong alkali, **d)** a very weak alkali.
8. **a)** What is the pH of water?
   **b)** What word is used to describe its degree of acidity or alkalinity?
9. Why is soap used to treat a bee sting and vinegar to treat a wasp sting?
10. What are the missing reactants and products in these reactions?

    **a)** _____ + sodium hydroxide → sodium chloride + _____

    **b)** hydrochloric acid + _____ → zinc chloride + _____

    **c)** What kind of reactions are **a)** and **b)**?

# 7 Air

## Answers

### Liquid air and the discovery of some noble gases (PB page 78)

1 Dust can be removed by filtration.
2 by cooling the air down to below 278°C
3 by 194 times atmospheric pressure
4 It is too cold.
5 M.W. Travers (krypton, neon and xenon)

### Uses of the air gases (PB page 82)

1 Yes. Nitrogen is an essential component of proteins from which we and all living things are made and which becomes available to plants from the air through the action of lightning. It is an unreactive gas and is used instead of air in packaging. It is used as a coolant and as a raw material for making ammonia and nitric acid for use in the chemical industry. Oxygen is needed for respiration, a vital process for living things. It allows burning which releases energy for a wide variety of uses. Argon is used in light bulbs, neon is used in advertising displays, helium is used in weather balloons and to help deep sea divers breathe. Krypton is used in airport landing lights and lighthouses. Xenon is used in a photographer's flash gun.

### Burning (PB page 83)

2 The answer should include these examples:

wood – camp fires in developed countries, vital fuel for cooking and heating in developing countries
coal – used in power stations and for heating some homes in country districts
coke – extraction of iron from its ore
charcoal – cooking food on barbecues
oil – used in power stations and some homes and factories for heating
diesel oil – used in trucks and some cars
petrol – used in most cars, all motor bikes and some lawnmowers
natural gas – in some power stations and for heating many homes and for use in cooking
wax – for candles to provide light or to keep meals warm on a dining table

### The danger of incomplete combustion (PB page 84)

3 The carbon does not form carbon dioxide but forms carbon monoxide. This is a result of incomplete combustion because there is not enough air passing through the fire to provide enough oxygen for complete combustion of the methane gas.

### The Bunsen burner (PB page 85)

4 Because the speed at which carbon reacts with oxygen is faster when the air hole is open than when it is closed.
5 Because less gas is delivered to the Bunsen burner.
6 Tie back long hair. Close the air hole before the burner is lit (this will make the flame easy to see when it is lit). Place the match to one side of the chimney to light the gas (otherwise the rush of gas may blow out the match). Do not put hands over the top of the Bunsen burner when it is lit (the skin may burn). The burner should have a small luminous flame when it is on but not being used for heating (the small flame produces less heat and does not wave about so much as a large flame, and the luminous flame is easy to see so that you can tell that the burner is ready for use). Remember that the size of the flame can be controlled by the gas tap (some people may try to change the size of a large flame by turning the regulator (collar) – this will only make a very hot roaring flame or a large luminous flame which may wave about due to air currents in the laboratory).

### Triangle of fire (PB page 86)

7 The sand forms a blanket over the fuel and prevents oxygen reaching it.

### Rise and fall of the phlogiston theory (PB page 88)

1 Some of the discoveries of the alchemists showed that some substances gained weight when combustion took place.
2 Hales devised a way of collecting gases over water.

# AIR

3 Black discovered that the same gas could be produced in different ways and that gases took part in chemical reactions.

4 a) The loss in volume of the air was due to Priestley's dephlogisticated air combining with the metal to form a calx.
  b) The change in weight was due to the dephlogisticated air combining with the metal to form the calx.

5 The metals combine with oxygen in the air and form oxides.

## Rust (PB page 90)

8 The walls would collapse. The steel would rust and become too weak to hold up the bricks and glass.

## End of chapter question (PB page 90)

1 It is true that air is a useful raw material because it provides nitrogen for fertilisers and, indirectly, food for us. Oxygen is a raw material for the combustion process which provides heat for a wide range of chemical reactions used in industry, such as the extraction of iron. The noble gases are extracted from the air and are used in the following ways: argon – light bulbs, neon – advertising displays, helium – weather balloons and to help deep sea divers breathe, krypton – airport landing lights and lighthouses, xenon – flash guns for photographic work. If other chapters have been studied which feature oxides, the use of oxygen in forming oxides may be mentioned. The main problem that air can create is in the production of fires due to combustion. However, this has to balanced against the presence of oxygen in the air allowing respiration to take place, which is a vital process.

## End of chapter test (WORKSHEET 7.2, TRB page 51)

1 a) nitrogen  b) argon  c) oxygen  d) neon
  e) nitrogen  f) oxygen  g) nitrogen
  h) helium
2 a substance that is burned to provide heat and light, e.g. natural gas, petrol, oil
3 methane + oxygen → carbon dioxide + water
4 a combustion reaction

5 Put a glowing splint into the gas and if it relights it is oxygen.

6 It combines with haemoglobin in the blood and prevents oxygen being carried to the cells. This can cause death.

7 When the air hole is opened more oxygen combines with the methane and a hotter flame is produced. The flame also changes from a silent luminous flame to a roaring non-luminous flame. When the air hole is closed less oxygen mixes with the gas and the flame returns to a luminous, silent and cooler flame.

8 If the gas tap is turned fully on, the largest flame is produced. If the gas tap is turned so as to close it a little, less gas passes to the burner and the flame is smaller.

9 to cool the material so much that it will not burn

10 Because the water sinks below the oil and then boils and bubbles through the oil, spraying it over a wide area. The oil can then start new fires or burn people close by.

11 It prevents water and oxygen reaching the surface of the metal. Both of these are needed for rusting to take place.

12 It combines with oxygen in the air to form an oxide layer on the surface. Oxygen cannot get to the metal beneath this layer so further reactions stop.

## IT input

Hall of Fame:

- Karl von Linde, PB page 78
- William Ramsay, PB page 78
- Georg Stahl, PB page 86
- Joannes Baptista van Helmont, PB page 86
- Stephen Hales, PB page 87
- Joseph Black, PB page 87
- Joseph Priestley, PB page 87
- Antoine Lavoisier, PB page 88

## Activities

### Activity 7.1 Burning candles 1

*Burning* (PB page 83) and *Test for water vapour* (PB page 62)

Ask the pupils to predict what would happen if a birthday cake candle was set alight and then covered by a beaker. Allow the pupils to check their prediction; ask how many groups performed the experiment more than once to check their results.

Present the pupils with a smaller and a larger beaker than the one they used previously and ask them to predict what will happen when a candle is burned in these. Allow them to test their ideas and at the end look for pupils' answers which record that the experiment has been repeated several times, with anomalous results identified and explained. Ask the pupils to plot a graph of their results and extrapolate and interpolate from their line with three points to predict how a candle will burn in smaller and larger beakers.

Extend by asking the pupils about any other observations they made while timing the burning candle. They should have observed that there appeared to be condensation inside the cold beaker and that they could test this with anhydrous copper sulphate (harmful) or anhydrous cobalt chloride (harmful). This is an example of scientists making discoveries which are not expected as they are not part of the plan of the experiment. This information can be used to identify a product of combustion.

**Preparation**

- For each class group: 250 cm$^3$, 100 cm$^3$ and 500 cm$^3$ beakers, birthday cake candle, Plasticine to hold the candle to the bench, stop clock

**Safety**

- Eye protection must be worn.
- Anhydrous copper sulphate and anhydrous cobalt chloride are harmful.

## Activity 7.2 Burning candles 2

### Burning (PB page 82)

The pupils are presented with a set of unassembled apparatus and asked to devise a way of using it to test for production of carbon dioxide when a candle burns. When the pupils have decided how to assemble the apparatus and predicted how it will work, they can be allowed to set up the apparatus and try the experiment.

This activity can also be used as an extension activity for pupils who finish other work early. They can demonstrate the procedure to the rest of the class.

**Preparation**

- For each class group: filter pump, two rubber tubes, boiling tube, stopper with two delivery tubes, thistle funnel, birthday cake candle, Plasticine, beaker of lime water

**Safety**

- Lime water is harmful.

## Activity 7.3 Investigating Bunsen burner flames

### The Bunsen burner (PB page 84)

Ask the pupils how they could compare the energy released by the different flames that can be produced by turning the air regulator (collar). In their plans, look for a certain volume of water being heated for a certain length of time and the recording of the first and final temperatures of the water.

**Preparation**

- For each class group: Bunsen burner, heatproof mat, tripod, gauze, measuring cylinder, beaker, thermometer, stop clock

**Safety**

- Eye protection must be worn.
- Make sure that the tripods have cooled down before clearing them away.

## Activity 7.4 Investigating rusting

### Rust (PB page 89)

WORKSHEET 7.1 Investigating rusting (TRB page 50)
Present the pupils with Worksheet 7.1 and go through it with them to check that they can relate the materials provided to generating the four conditions for the experiment, and then let them plan and set up their investigation. Allow the pupils supervised access to their investigation every three days so they can check for signs of rust and compare the speed of rusting.

**Preparation**

- For each class group: four test-tubes, test-tube stopper, four iron nails
- Chemicals: salt solution, boiled water, anhydrous calcium chloride, oil

**Safety**

- Eye protection must be worn.
- Calcium chloride is an irritant.

## AIR

# WORKSHEET 7.1   *Investigating rusting*

 Eye protection must be worn

 Calcium chloride is an irritant – handle it with care

You are provided with:

- four test-tubes
- a test-tube stopper
- four iron nails
- salt solution
- water
- boiled water
- a drying agent (anhydrous calcium chloride (irritant))
- oil

Use these to set up test-tubes in which there are the following conditions:

1. air and water
2. air, salt and water
3. air and no water
4. water and no air

Explain how these can safely be used to test the conditions needed for rusting to occur.

Predict which nail will rust the most.

Carry out the test to see if your prediction is correct.

# WORKSHEET 7.2   *End of chapter test*

1. What gas in the air **a)** forms the major part of the air, **b)** is used in light bulbs, **c)** is used in respiration, **d)** is used in advertising, **e)** is used in making fertiliser, **f)** is used to burn fuels in rockets, **g)** is used to cool and store biological material, **h)** is used in weather balloons?
2. What is a fuel? Give three examples.
3. Rearrange these substances to form the equation which describes what happens when methane burns in air:

    carbon dioxide    oxygen    water    methane

4. Is the reaction in question 3 **i)** a decomposition reaction, **ii)** a combustion reaction, or **iii)** a displacement reaction?
5. What is the test for oxygen?
6. Why is carbon monoxide dangerous?
7. How does opening and closing the air hole on a Bunsen burner affect the flame?
8. How can the gas tap be used to control the flame?
9. Why is water poured onto a fire to put it out?
10. Why must water not be poured onto burning oil?
11. Why does painting steel stop it rusting?
12. Why does aluminium not rust?

---

# WORKSHEET 7.2   *End of chapter test*

1. What gas in the air **a)** forms the major part of the air, **b)** is used in light bulbs, **c)** is used in respiration, **d)** is used in advertising, **e)** is used in making fertiliser, **f)** is used to burn fuels in rockets, **g)** is used to cool and store biological material, **h)** is used in weather balloons?
2. What is a fuel? Give three examples.
3. Rearrange these substances to form the equation which describes what happens when methane burns in air:

    carbon dioxide    oxygen    water    methane

4. Is the reaction in question 3 **i)** a decomposition reaction, **ii)** a combustion reaction, or **iii)** a displacement reaction?
5. What is the test for oxygen?
6. Why is carbon monoxide dangerous?
7. How does opening and closing the air hole on a Bunsen burner affect the flame?
8. How can the gas tap be used to control the flame?
9. Why is water poured onto a fire to put it out?
10. Why must water not be poured onto burning oil?
11. Why does painting steel stop it rusting?
12. Why does aluminium not rust?

# 8 The Earth — a rocky planet

## Answers

### The Earth's structure (PB page 92)

1 Radioactive materials like uranium are present. The radiation from these materials heats the inside of the Earth.
2 The temperature would fall.
3 Magma is molten rock. It reaches the surface because it is lighter than the solid rock and flows upwards between the crystals.

### Volcanoes (PB page 94)

4 The dust spreads out into the atmosphere and scatters the different colours in sunlight. If the pupils have covered dispersion in their physics course they may add that when the sun is low on the horizon it shines through a thicker layer of the atmosphere than when it is higher in the sky. The light will shine through a thicker layer of dust and the colours will be dispersed more.
5 a) They both produce lava and have a vent.
  b) Andesitic volcanoes are cone shaped and form above ground; they produce a thick lava; they do not form on hot spots. Basaltic volcanoes are shield shaped and usually form under water; they produce a thinner lava and form over hot spots.
6 There are gases inside the rock. When the rock escapes from the volcano the pressure on the gases is reduced and they expand and make bubbles which are later seen as holes. The pupils may visualise this more easily if they have investigated dough in their biology course.

### Igneous rock (PB page 95)

7 They form from molten rocks which glow.
8 An extrusive igneous rock is one that reaches the Earth's surface, e.g. basalt. An intrusive igneous rock is one that rises into the Earth's crust but does not reach the Earth's surface, e.g. granite.
9 An extrusive rock has small crystals because it cooled down quickly and an intrusive rock has large crystals because it cooled down slowly.

10 a) Granite is hard and is not easily broken up by pressure.
  b) The surface of granite can be polished to a smooth finish and the large colourful and differently shaped crystals make the rock attractive.

### Minerals (PB page 96)

1 a substance formed from one or more elements in the Earth
2  1 a) mineral does not have colour.....................rock crystal
     b) mineral has colour..........see 2
   2 a) mineral is white..............milky quartz
     b) mineral is not white .......see 3
   3 a) mineral is pink................rose quartz
     b) mineral is not pink.........see 4
   4 a) mineral is purple............amethyst
     b) mineral is black..............smoky quartz
3 Gemstones have a pleasing colour or a shiny surface, or sparkle when light passes through them.
4 Yes – gemstones are minerals because they are made from one or more elements in the Earth's crust.

### Sedimentary rock (PB page 98)

11 All three kinds of sedimentary rock form by solid particles settling down together, but the source of the particles is different in each case. Sandstone, for example, is formed from particles from weathered rocks. Limestone is formed from particles of substances such as shells that have been made by living things. Rock salt and gypsum form from the chemicals dissolved in sea water when the sea water dries up.
12 The rocks form in layers, which allows them to be easily broken up into pieces that are the right size for building stones.

### Metamorphic rock (PB page 99)

13 a change of form
14 pressure or a rise in temperature
15 marble, which has a sugar-like texture with streaks of colourful materials
16 It forms lightweight sheets and does not let water pass through it.

# ANSWERS

## Physical weathering (PB page 100)

**17** It may have been chipped off a rock surface by a piece of grit or another grain of sand. It may have broken off from a rock by the pushing and pulling forces due to expansion and contraction during the heat of the day and the cool of the night. It may have been broken off a piece of rock by water entering a crack and freezing – the expansion of the water as it turned to ice broke off a piece of rock.

## Chemical weathering (PB page 101)

**18** in limestone rocks

**19** The acidic solution made by carbon dioxide dissolving in rain water reacts with carbonates in limestone and results in holes being made. The sulphuric acid in acid rain causes calcium and magnesium sulphate crystals to form, which in time cause part of the rock to crumble.

## Completing the rock cycle (PB page 103)

**20** The sedimentary rock is taken back under the crust to form magma or it is turned into a metamorphic rock which in time goes to form magma. The magma forms extrusive igneous rock which is weathered to form sedimentary rock again.

**21** Another arrow can be drawn from igneous rock (extrusive) to metamorphic rock.

## End of chapter question (PB page 103)

**1** The slate formed from igneous rock that weathered and formed particles. These stuck together to form a sedimentary rock which was then heated and squashed to form the slate.

Magma rose up through the crust but did not reach the surface. It cooled slowly in the crust to form granite.

In ancient seas, sea creatures made shells and then died. The shells collected at the bottom of the sea and formed limestone. This was heated and squashed to form marble.

The sandstone formed from igneous rock which has weathered and produced small particles.

## End of chapter test (WORKSHEET 8.1, TRB page 56)

**1**

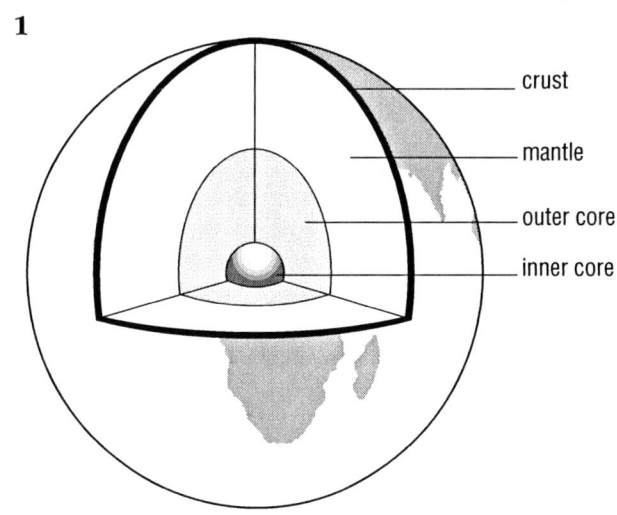

**2**

|  | Examples |
|---|---|
| igneous rocks | granite and basalt |
| metamorphic rocks | marble and slate |
| sedimentary rocks | sandstone and limestone |

**3** granite and basalt

**4** sandstone

**5** slate and marble

**6** A rock that cools slowly has large crystals and a rock that cools quickly has small crystals.

**7 a)** granite
   **b)** Granite cools down more slowly than basalt.

**8** limestone

**9** sedimentary rocks

**10 a)** The ice will expand and put such pressure on the rock that parts of the rock snap off.
   **b)** physical weathering

**11**

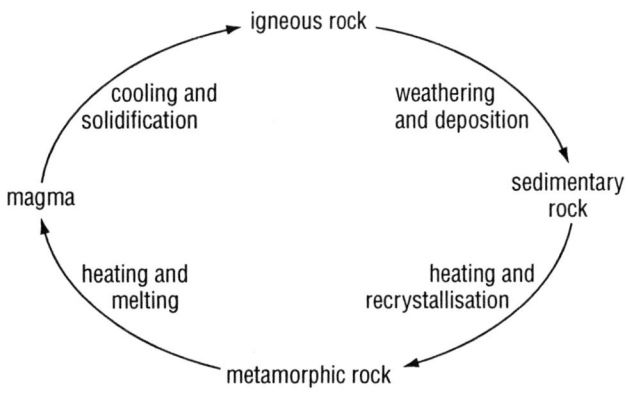

Chemistry Now! 11–14 Teacher's Resource Book

# THE EARTH – A ROCKY PLANET

## IT input

Hall of Fame:

- Friedrich Mohs, TRB page 55

Pupils can use CD-ROMs and the Internet to search for information on minerals.

## Activities

### Activity 8.1  A rock key

**Types of rock** (PB page 95)

Present each group with a selection of rocks and ask them to produce a rock key based on their observations. When the rock key has been made, take away the specimens the pupils have used and present them with a few other specimens and ask them to classify them.

Extend the activity by presenting the pupils with a piece of granite with xenoliths and asking them to comment on its structure. Look for answers which state that there is a second rock embedded in the granite.

Extend further by presenting the pupils with a piece of conglomerate and asking them to comment on its structure. Look for answers which state that it is formed from pieces of different rock that have become cemented together in sedimentary rock.

**Preparation**

- Rock specimens for the pupils: biotite granite, olivine basalt, slate, marble, sandstone, crinoid limestone
- 'Challenge' specimens, e.g. hornblende biotite granite, serpentine marble, shelly limestone, gritstone
- Extension specimens: granite with xenoliths, conglomerate

### Activity 8.2  Investigating how ice affects pumice stone

**How rock breaks up** (PB page 99)

Give the pupils a sample of pumice stone and ask them to predict what would happen if ice formed in the cavities in it. Ask the pupils to plan an investigation to test their idea and check that it includes two pieces of pumice stone (one which will be frozen and one which will not be frozen, for comparison) before they proceed. The pupils may be surprised to find that the pumice stone floats, and may have to revise their plan to include placing a weight over the pumice stone in the water while the water freezes. Arrange for the stones in their containers of water to be placed in a deep freeze until the next lesson. Arrange for the samples to be taken out of the deep freeze some time before the lesson so that the ice can have begun to melt. Let the pupils look for signs of weathering as they compare the two stones and describe what they find.

**Preparation**

- For each class group: two pieces of pumice stone, a metal dish, a weight (mass)
- The stones in the dishes of water will have to be stored in a deep freeze until the water has frozen

### Activity 8.3  Polarised light

**Minerals** (PB page 96)

Introduce the use of polarised light by saying that the light is filtered so that only light waves in one plane pass through the transparent crystals and when they do they are split by the arrangement of atoms in the crystal. When the light passes through the upper piece of polarising material it may form colours which can be used to identify the mineral.

This activity is designed to show that polarised light can be used in the examination and identification of minerals. Two small pieces of polarising material are set up, one below the microscope slide and one above it. The upper sheet is turned so that the light polarised by the lower sheet does not pass through it. Some of the light passing through the substances on the slide is deflected so that it passes through the upper polarising sheet and the colourful images of some of the substances can be seen when examined with the microscope.

Let the pupils investigate the effects of polarised light on different specimens and describe what they see.

# ACTIVITIES

**Preparation**
- For each class group: microscope, microscope slides, two pieces of polarising material, salt, sand, sugar, calcite, a prepared slide of a rock sample

**Safety**
- If polarising material is cut from sheets, ensure that sharp edges are covered, for example by tape.

## Activity 8.4 Investigating the hardness of minerals

### *Minerals* (PB page 96)

Friedrich Mohs (1773–1839) was a German scientist who studied minerals and invented a scale of hardness which could be used in their identification. He arranged minerals on a ten-point scale, giving the softest a value of 1 and the hardest a value of 10. (These values cannot be calibrated in SI units.) Each mineral in the scale can be scratched by the one above it in the scale and can scratch the one below it. Introduce this information to the pupils and then let them investigate samples of quartz, gypsum, calcite, fluorite, apatite and feldspar and see if they can arrange them in the correct order in the scale (which is gypsum 2, calcite 3, fluorite 4, apatite 5, feldspar 6, quartz 7).

Extend by introducing talc and asking the pupils to assign it to a position on the scale. (It is position 1.)

**Preparation**
- For each class group: samples of gypsum, calcite, fluorite, apatite, feldspar, quartz and talc

**Safety**
- Eye protection must be worn.

THE EARTH – A ROCKY PLANET

# WORKSHEET 8.1  *End of chapter test*

1. Make a labelled diagram to show the structure of the Earth.
2. Fill in the table using the rocks in this list:

    basalt    limestone    marble    granite    slate    sandstone

    |  | Examples |
    |---|---|
    | igneous rocks |  |
    | metamorphic rocks |  |
    | sedimentary rocks |  |

3. Which rocks in the table have formed directly from magma?
4. Which rock in the table has formed directly from small pieces of other rock?
5. Which rocks in the table have formed from rocks that have been squashed and heated?
6. How does the speed of cooling of a rock affect the size of the crystals that form in it?
7. a) Which rock – granite or basalt – has the larger crystals?
   b) What does the size of the crystals in the two rocks tell you about the way the rocks formed?
8. Which rock in the table has formed from the shells of sea creatures?
9. A rock is discovered which appears to have formed from chemicals that were left behind when a sea dried up. Into which group in the table should it be placed?
10. a) Water fills a crack in a rock and then freezes. How may this affect the rock?
    b) Is this an example of physical or chemical weathering?
11. Redraw this rock cycle with the arrows in the correct places:

    igneous rock

    magma                    sedimentary rock

    metamorphic rock

    cooling and solidification →       weathering and deposition →

    heating and melting →              heating and recrystallisation →

# 9 Metals and non-metals

## Answers

### Physical properties (PB page 105)

1 Some elements have exceptional properties. Mercury, for instance, is a liquid at room temperature like some of the non-metals. Iodine looks like metal, having a shiny metallic appearance, but is a non-metal. Carbon in its graphite form conducts electricity like metals.

### Chemical properties (PB page 106)

2 When a metal reacts with oxygen a metal oxide is formed which may react with an acid to form a salt and water. Some metal oxides are soluble in water and are called alkalis. An alkali can be identified using universal indicator paper (which turns light blue or dark blue) or by red litmus paper (which turns blue). When a non-metal takes part in a chemical reaction with oxygen an oxide is also formed. Most non-metal oxides are soluble in water and dissolve in it to form acids. These turn universal indicator paper red or yellow and turn blue litmus paper red.

3 a) Carbon forms an oxide which dissolves in water and forms a solution which has a pH of 5. This is acidic and shows the oxide to be that of a non-metal.

b) Magnesium forms an oxide which dissolves in water to form a solution which is pH 8. This is alkaline and shows the oxide to be that of a metal.

### Reaction with oxygen (PB page 107)

4 sodium, iron, copper, gold

### Reaction with water (PB page 108)

5 potassium, sodium, calcium, magnesium, iron, copper
6 potassium, sodium, calcium, magnesium
7 potassium, sodium
8 a metal oxide
9 It would react with the hot water.

### Reaction with acids (PB page 109)

10 magnesium, zinc, iron, lead, copper

11 There were more acid 'particles' (or ions) with which the metal could react.
12 It would react much faster.
13 metal + hydrochloric acid
   → metal chloride + hydrogen

### Displacement reactions (PB page 110)

14 iron, copper, silver

### The reactivity series (PB page 110)

15 Zinc oxide forms more quickly than iron oxide. The answer should not say 'very vigorously', as the pupils should understand that the table is showing trends. Zinc and iron both produce hydrogen with steam. The rate of reaction between zinc and the acid is faster than the reaction between iron and the acid.
16 a) Yes – it is more reactive than iron.
   b) Yes – it is more reactive than lead.
   c) No – it is less reactive than aluminium.

### Generating electricity with metals (PB page 111)

17 To show that a current of electricity is being generated. Some of the electrical energy is being converted into light energy.
18 The voltage depends on the gap between the two metals in the reactivity series. As the gap between the two metals increases the voltage becomes larger.

### The dry cell (PB page 112)

19 The liquids may spill or leak from the container. The chemicals in a dry cell will not spill or leak.
20 The chemicals taking part in the reaction are eventually used up.

### How electricity came to be used in chemistry (PB page 113)

1 Priestley wrote a book about the work of scientists studying electricity. When Volta read the book he became interested in electricity and developed a battery which Nicholson and Carlisle used to split up water into its elements. When Davy had studied their work he also used a voltaic pile to discover new elements.

# METALS AND NON-METALS

2 The copper and iron generated electricity in some way.

3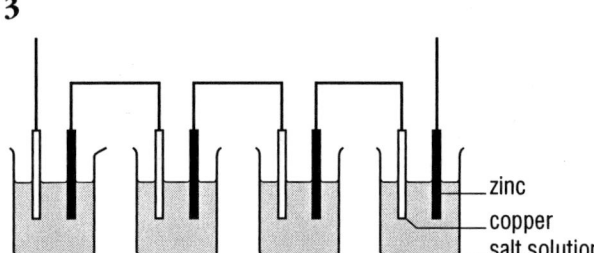

4 It was more compact – a larger number of cells could be set up in the same space as a row of bowls and metal strips.

5 Electricity could be used to produce chemical reactions. (This has been used to show how simple chemicals found in living things can be produced by using a spark in a mixture of gases.)

6 potassium, sodium, magnesium, calcium, strontium, barium

## Solutions (PB page 115)

21 salt from the sweat

## Electrolysis (PB pages 115 and 117)

22 It is a solution or molten solid through which a current passes, e.g. molten sodium chloride, copper sulphate solution, sodium chloride solution, sulphuric acid, sodium hydroxide solution.

23 a) magnesium   b) copper

24 a) potassium, sodium, calcium, magnesium, aluminium, zinc, iron, tin, lead
   b) copper, silver, gold

## Extraction of metals (PB page 118)

25 It costs money to use energy, so any reduction in the amount of energy needed to melt the raw material will make the product cheaper.

## Electroplating (PB page 118)

26 Copper has come out of solution and settled on the cathode and increased the cathode's mass.

27 Some of the copper has dissolved in the electrolyte and the mass of the anode has fallen.

## End of chapter questions (PB page 119)

1 The reactivity series is a list of metals arranged in order of their reactivity, starting with the most reactive. It can be used to compare the reactivities of metals and to make predictions about how metals will react together, what the outcome of a displacement reaction might be, and what voltage is likely to be produced when the two metals are used in a cell.

2 Chemical reactions between different metals in a solution such as sodium chloride solution can be used to generate electricity. Hydrogen bubbles would stop the flow of electricity in a dry cell, and complicated chemical reactions take place to remove them.

3 Electricity can be used to separate copper and oxygen in a solution of copper sulphate, hydrogen and oxygen from a solution of magnesium sulphate or hydrogen and chlorine from brine, or it can be used with heat energy to separate sodium and chlorine from molten salt or lead and bromine from lead bromide.

## End of chapter test (WORKSHEET 9.5, TRB page 66)

1 a) non-metal   b) metal   c) non-metal
  d) metal   e) non-metal   f) metal   g) metal
  h) metal   i) non-metal

2 non-metal

3 a) zinc + sulphur → zinc sulphide
  b) a synthesis reaction

4 a) turn it blue   b) unchanged
  It is an alkali.

5 a) unchanged   b) turn it red
  It is an acid.

6 a) B, D, C, A   b) i) A   ii) B   iii) D   iv) C

7 a) iron + copper sulphate
     → iron sulphate + copper
  b) a displacement reaction

8 a)

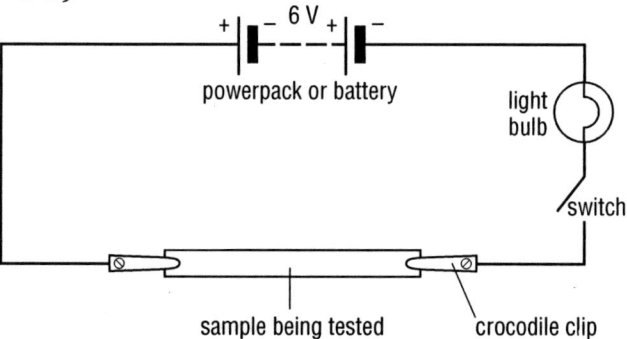

If pupils have done work involving ammeters in the physics course, they may draw an ammeter in place of a lamp.

b) The lamp or LED would not light.

9 Bromine gas is produced at the anode and lead is produced at the cathode.

**10 a), b)**

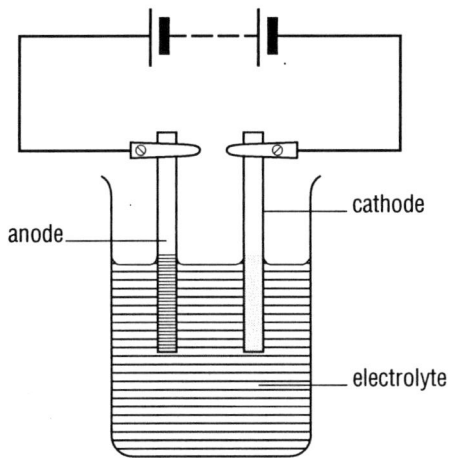

c) The metal at the anode dissolves in the electrolyte and the metal in the electrolyte comes out of solution on the cathode and forms a coating.

# IT input

Hall of Fame:

- Joseph Priestley, PB page 112
- Alessandro Volta, PB page 112
- Luigi Galvani, PB page 112
- William Nicholson, PB page 113
- Anthony Carlisle, PB page 113
- Humphry Davy, PB page 113
- Michael Faraday, PB page 113

# Activities

## Activity 9.1 Properties of metals and non-metals

### *Physical properties* (PB page 104)

WORKSHEET 9.1 Metals and non-metals (TRB page 62)

This activity provides a useful exercise in observation. Many pupils do not observe well enough and tend to think chemistry is purely a theoretical subject; it is not, and getting them thinking about what is happening at the atomic scale, even at this stage, will prepare them well for future studies. As they are observing the difference between metals and non-metals it may be useful to explain, simplistically, why these elements differ.

Note that the preparation details given below are just a guide. It will be your discretion and your availability of materials that determine which substances can be tested.

**Preparation**

- For each class group: leads and crocodile clips, ammeter, battery supply
- Metals: it may be useful to have metals which oxidise easily, for example magnesium, to show that it is dull but may be polished to give a shiny surface, and metals which do not, for example copper. Others may be sodium under oil, zinc, gold or silver jewellery, mercury, aluminium.
- Non-metals: a range is useful such as sulphur, bromine, carbon, nitrogen and oxygen (in the air)

**Safety**

- Eye protection must be worn.
- Do not allow pupils to test mercury, bromine, nitrogen or oxygen in an electrical circuit.
- Do not let pupils handle the very reactive elements: sodium, lithium, bromine or mercury. These should not be used in any way other than observation.
- Sulphur is an irritant.
- Bromine is harmful if ingested.
- Mercury is toxic if ingested.

## Activity 9.2 Investigating the oxides of metals and non-metals

### *Reaction with oxygen* (PB page 105)

Once the physical properties of metals and non-metals have been characterised, the pupils may look at the oxides of metals and non-metals. They can burn the element in oxygen and then dissolve the product in water to give a solution. A study of the alkalinity or acidity of the oxides can be performed.

This could be a full investigation. The teacher should demonstrate sodium, lithium and potassium, as these are very reactive metals. The pupils will have to decide the best way of burning the other elements. Some are easy, for example the burning of magnesium has already been studied in Activity 5.1. Some will be more difficult, for example sulphur, but pupils can use the investigation sheets to plan their experiments. A useful way of testing the oxide of sulphur is to burn sulphur in a test-tube and place a delivery

# METALS AND NON-METALS

tube from the test-tube into a test-tube of water with universal indicator solution in it. As the sulphur dioxide is produced and bubbles through the water, the colour will change from green to red.

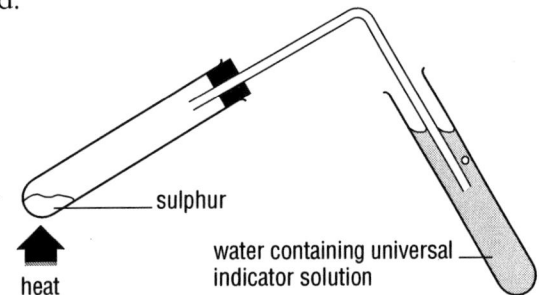

### Preparation
- For each class group: beakers, test-tubes, test-tube rack, bung with delivery tube attached, Bunsen burner
- Chemicals: calcium, magnesium, sulphur (very small amounts), universal indicator solution

### Safety
- Eye protection must be worn.
- Sulphur must be burned in a fume cupboard to allow ventilation.

## Activity 9.3 Investigating the reactivity series

### *The reactivity series* (PB page 110)

This is covered in Activities 5.3 and 6.5. These two practicals may be tied together to give an investigation into the reactivity series and to enable the pupils to conclude for themselves the order of increasing reactivity of the metals in the periodic table.

### Preparation
- For each class group: test-tubes, conical flask, bung with delivery tube, glass wool, 250 cm$^3$ graduated syringe, stop clock, dropping funnel, water bath, test-tubes, splints
- Chemicals: aqueous (1.0 M) solutions of copper sulphate, magnesium sulphate and iron sulphate, 0.4 M hydrochloric acid
- Metals: strips of copper, zinc, magnesium and iron

### Safety
- Eye protection must be worn.
- Copper sulphate, magnesium sulphate and iron sulphate solutions are harmful to the eyes and skin – remove any by washing immediately.

## Activity 9.4 Reaction of metals with water or steam

### *Reaction with water* (PB page 107)

WORKSHEET 9.2 Reaction of metals with water or steam (TRB page 63)

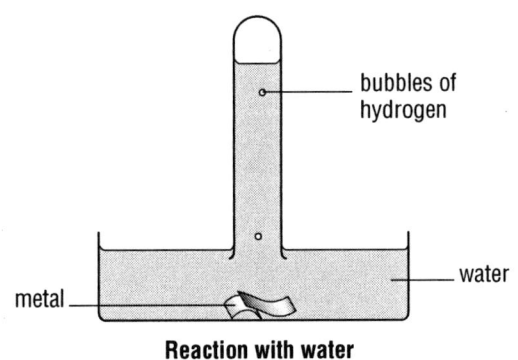
**Reaction with water**

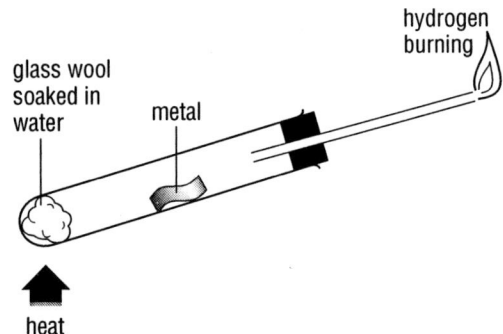
**Reaction with steam**

Metals react with water to produce the hydroxides, giving alkaline solutions. Depending upon the reactivity (studied in Activity 9.3), the metals may react very vigorously or very slowly with water. The reactions of the alkali metals (group I) may be done as a teacher demonstration, since the reactions of lithium, sodium and potassium with water are very vigorous and must be performed behind a screen using a large water bath. As in Activity 9.2, some universal indicator may be added to the water to show the production of an alkaline solution, going from green to blue. Some metals require steam to react since their reaction with water is slow.

### Preparation
- For the teacher demonstration: water bath, screen
- Metals for the teacher: lithium, sodium, potassium under oil. The oil may be removed immediately prior to use by washing with a little hexane or petroleum spirit (flammable); this aids reaction

60 CHEMISTRY NOW! 11–14 Teacher's Resource Book

# ACTIVITIES

- For each class group: beaker, glass wool, test-tubes and bungs, glass tubing, boiling tube and bung with hole
- Metals: zinc, magnesium, iron, copper

**Safety**

- Eye protection must be worn.
- Lithium, sodium and potassium are flammable, corrosive and cause burns. The alkaline solutions they produce with water are caustic.

## Activity 9.5 Electrolysis

### *Electrolysis* (PB page 115)

WORKSHEET 9.3 Electrolysis (TRB page 64)

This is a topic which many pupils find difficult. At this level it is important that pupils do not feel disheartened by the subject and it should be made very straightforward. It is important to study this after the reactivity series of metals, as the pupils will then be able to appreciate the difference in the reactions. If copper is used, it will be deposited on the electrode (the cathode) because it is a relatively unreactive metal whereas, because magnesium is more reactive, the actual electrolyte is water and hydrogen will be produced at the cathode so that the more reactive metal can stay in solution. The pupils are developing practical skills and understanding of the subject matter.

### Preparation

- For each class group: carbon electrodes, 6 V battery, leads and crocodile clips
- Chemicals: 1 M copper sulphate solution, 1 M magnesium sulphate solution

**Safety**

- Eye protection must be worn.
- Copper sulphate and magnesium sulphate solutions are harmful to the eyes and skin – remove any by washing immediately.

## Activity 9.6 Electroplating

### *Electroplating* (PB page 118)

WORKSHEET 9.4 Electroplating (TRB page 65)

This activity is always popular with pupils. They may choose to electroplate anything they wish. They are developing an understanding of the chemistry of electrolysis reactions and they are increasing their practical skills.

This practical could easily be used as an investigation into the factors influencing the speed and amount of electroplating. The investigation sheets may be used for this purpose.

The apparatus is set up as shown on the worksheet. The rheostat controls the current flowing through the circuit. The pupils can record the mass of nickel deposited for different current values over a set period of time by recording the mass of the electrodes before and after electrolysis. The electrodes may be cleaned by rinsing with water, followed with alcohol.

### Preparation

- For each class group: copper and nickel electrodes, 6 V battery, leads and crocodile clips, rheostat, stop clock
- Chemicals: 0.5 M nickel sulphate solution, ethanol

**Safety**

- Eye protection must be worn.
- Nickel sulphate is harmful by ingestion and solutions should be handled with gloves.
- Ethanol is highly flammable and is irritating to the eyes.

# METALS AND NON-METALS

## WORKSHEET 9.1   *Metals and non-metals*

 Eye protection must be worn

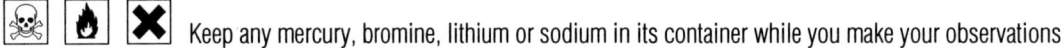 Keep any mercury, bromine, lithium or sodium in its container while you make your observations

1. Construct a table in the space below to show the properties of the elements. Include properties such as colour, shininess, malleability (will it bend or does it crumble?), what state it is in (solid, liquid or gas?).
2. Test the electrical conductivity of the elements supplied by your teacher by including them in an electrical circuit. Connect leads with crocodile clips to an ammeter and battery. Include the element as part of the circuit by attaching crocodile clips, and see whether it conducts electricity. (This will be shown by a reading on the ammeter.) Construct a table of your results.

# WORKSHEET 9.2 *Reaction of metals with water or steam*

**Eye protection must be worn**

1. Fill a test-tube with water and stopper it.
2. Place 100 cm³ of water in a water bath and add the metal. If any bubbles form, collect the gas by holding the inverted test-tube full of water over the bubbles.

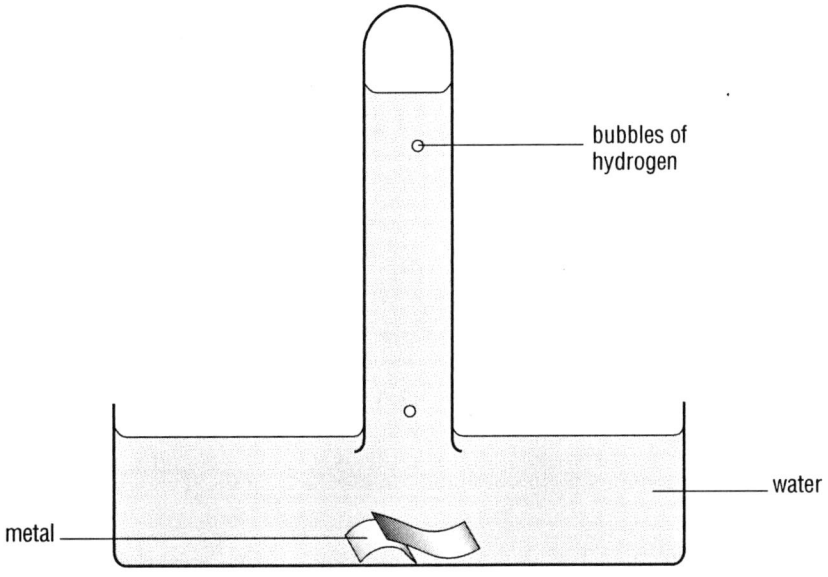

3. Any metals which show little or no reaction with water can be used for reaction with steam. Using tongs, place glass wool soaked in water into the bottom of a boiling tube. Place the metal in the middle of the boiling tube. Stopper the boiling tube using a bung with a piece of glass tubing through it.

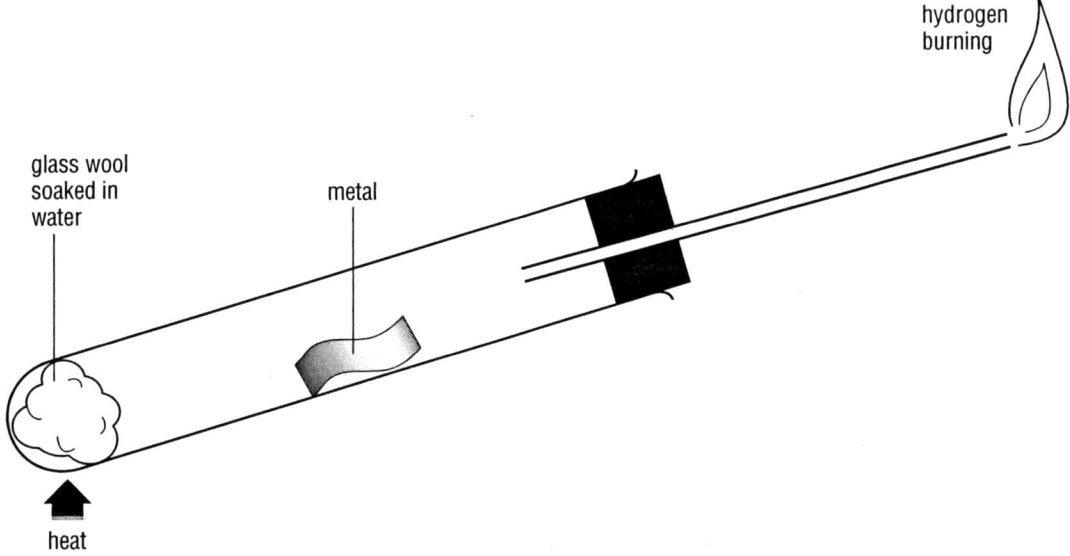

4. Heat the metal until it starts to glow or melt and then heat the glass wool to produce steam. The reaction will start to occur.
5. Light the hydrogen produced at the glass tube protruding from the boiling tube.

**METALS AND NON-METALS**

# WORKSHEET 9.3  *Electrolysis*

👁 Eye protection must be worn

✖ Handle copper sulphate and magnesium sulphate solutions with great care

1  Set up the apparatus as shown in the diagram.

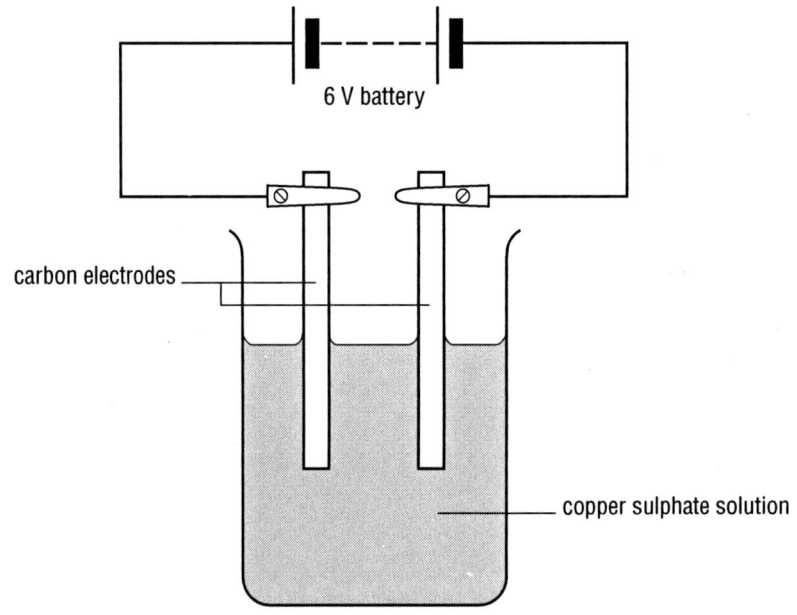

2  Leave the apparatus for about 15 minutes.
3  Repeat the experiment using magnesium sulphate solution.

**Questions**

1  What do you observe at the electrodes? If a gas is given off, where do you think it has come from? What gas could it be?

2  Is there any difference in the intensity of colour of the copper sulphate solution?

3  Is there any metal in the bottom of the beaker? What metal do you think it is?

**METALS AND NON-METALS**

# WORKSHEET 9.4 *Electroplating*

 Eye protection must be worn

 Handle nickel sulphate solution with great care

1. Set up the apparatus as shown in the diagram.
2. Allow the current to flow until the nickel has plated the copper electrode.
3. Explain what is happening.

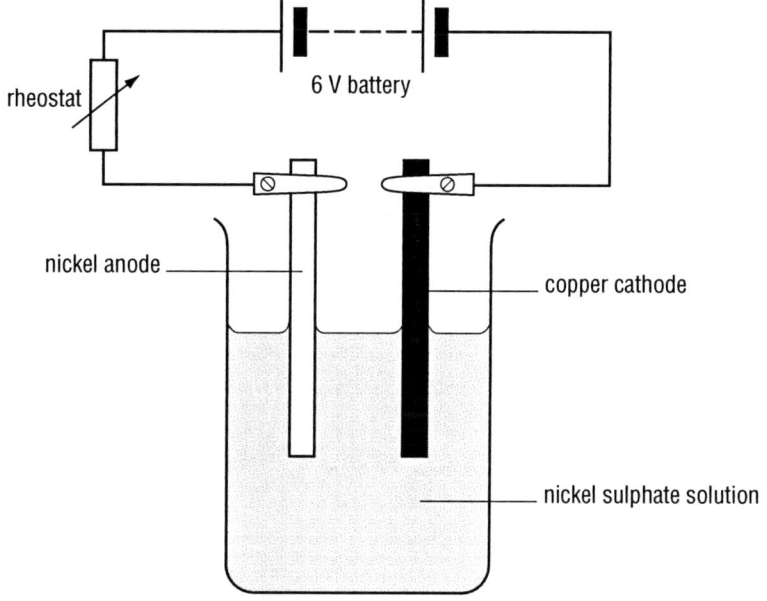

---

# WORKSHEET 9.4 *Electroplating*

 Eye protection must be worn

 Handle nickel sulphate solution with great care

1. Set up the apparatus as shown in the diagram.
2. Allow the current to flow until the nickel has plated the copper electrode.
3. Explain what is happening.

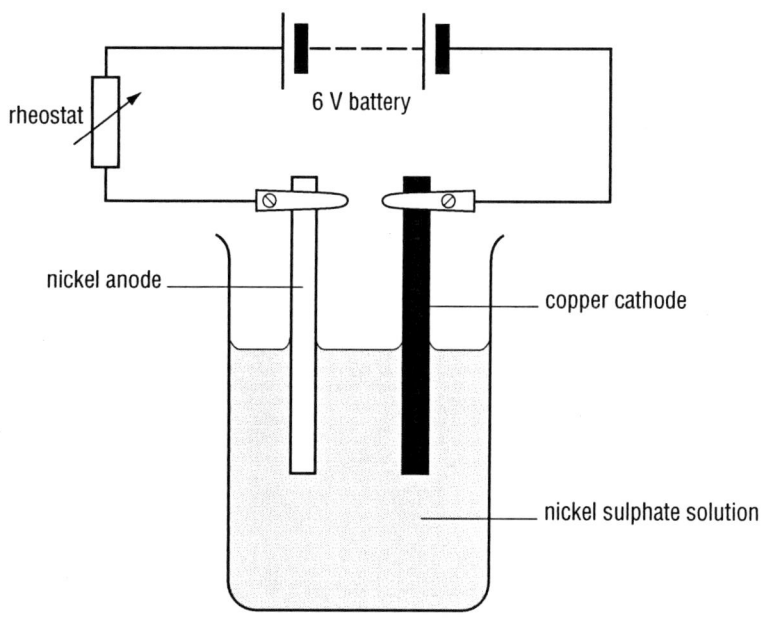

© John Murray — Chemistry Now! 11–14 Teacher's Resource Book

# METALS AND NON-METALS

## WORKSHEET 9.5  *End of chapter test*

1. Does a metal or a non-metal **a)** have a low density, **b)** have a shiny surface, **c)** have a low melting point, **d)** have a high boiling point, **e)** break easily when hammered, **f)** ring when tapped, **g)** have great strength, **h)** conduct heat, **i)** prevent electricity passing through it?

2. An element in a test-tube at room temperature is a gas. Is it a metal or a non-metal?

3. **a)** Complete this word equation:

    zinc + _____ → zinc sulphide

    **b)** Is the reaction **i)** an oxidation, **ii)** a synthesis, or **iii)** a decomposition reaction?

4. A metal oxide dissolves in water. How will it affect **a)** red litmus paper, **b)** blue litmus paper? Explain your answer.

5. A non-metal oxide dissolves in water. How will it affect **a)** red litmus paper, **b)** blue litmus paper? Explain your answer.

6. Metal A does not react with oxygen, water, steam or acid. Metal B reacts with oxygen very vigorously, produces hydrogen with cold water and has a violent reaction with acid. Metal C reacts very slowly with oxygen, does not react with steam and only reacts very slowly with acid. Metal D reacts slowly with oxygen, produces hydrogen from steam but not from water, and reacts slowly with acid.

    **a)** Arrange the metals in order of reactivity, starting with the most reactive.

    **b)** Which metal could be **i)** gold, **ii)** potassium, **iii)** iron, **iv)** lead?

7. **a)** Complete this word equation:

    iron + copper sulphate → _____ + _____

    **b)** What kind of reaction is it?

8. **a)** Draw and label a circuit that you would set up to test whether a material was a conductor of electricity.

    **b)** How could you tell if the material was an electrical insulator?

9. What happens to molten lead bromide when a current of electricity is passed through it? Use the words anode and cathode in your answer.

10. The diagram shows a cell set up for electroplating.

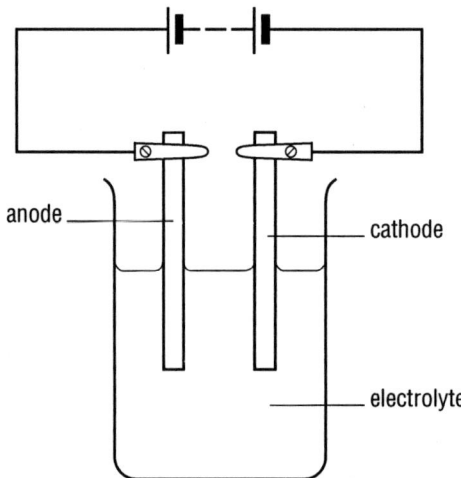

   **a)** Shade in the part which is to be electroplated.

   **b)** Draw horizontal lines through the part or parts which contain the metal that is to form the coating.

   **c)** What happens when the current is switched on?

# 10 Earth materials

## Answers

### Gold (PB page 122)
1. **a)** 91.6%, **b)** 58.3%, **c)** 37.5% gold
2. To make a metal that looks like gold but is cheaper. (It also allows an amount of gold to make more objects with a gold appearance than if pure gold was used.)

### Silver (PB page 123)
3. Sterling silver is harder than pure silver and will make sharper knives, and the prongs of forks will be less prone to bending.

### Copper (PB pages 124 and 125)
4. concentration of the ore, roasting of the ore and electrolysis
5. iron, silver and gold
6. It pulls into a wire and conducts electricity well.
7. It is stronger than copper and will not be damaged by being pushed into plug sockets and pulled out again.

### Lead (PB page 125)
8. The flotation cell is used in the extraction of both metals. Copper ore is roasted in a furnace; lead ore is heated in a blast furnace then roasted in air. Both metals are purified in an electrical cell.
9. Lead is much heavier because it has a very high density.

### Iron (PB page 127)
10.

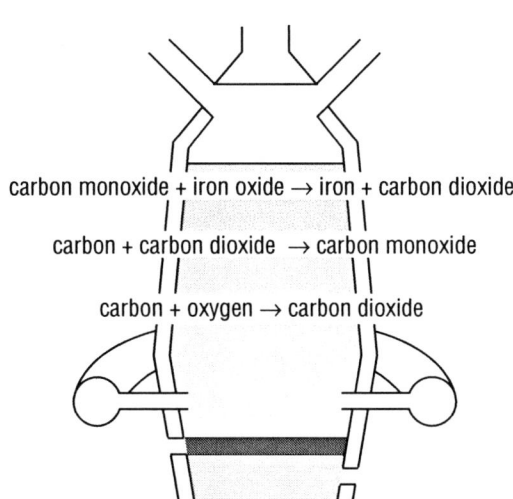

carbon monoxide + iron oxide → iron + carbon dioxide

carbon + carbon dioxide → carbon monoxide

carbon + oxygen → carbon dioxide

11. The rocky substance silicon oxide does not melt at the temperature in the furnace. Limestone is added because it breaks down to form calcium oxide, which combines with silicon oxide to form calcium silicate or slag. This substance melts at the temperature in the furnace and flows out with the iron.
12. 36 500 000 tonnes plus either 20 000 or 30 000 tonnes (depending on whether there were two or three leap years in the ten-year period).
13. Less fuel is needed to provide heat energy.
14. From the jet of air introduced into the bottom of the furnace.

### Early iron workers (PB page 128)
1. The armies of those countries that had iron would beat the armies of those countries that had bronze because the iron swords were stronger and the soldiers would not need to stop in battle to straighten them.
2. oxygen
3. It provided more oxygen to the hot metal ore.
4. iron and carbon
5. The Hittites discovered how to give wrought iron a steel coating. In Northern India it was discovered how to make wrought iron rustproof.

### Steel (PB page 130)
15. The metal would break because cast iron is brittle.
16. To prevent the metal from melting.
17. It is alloyed with nickel and chromium to make stainless steel.

### Zinc (PB page 131)
18. Iron is extracted by carbon monoxide removing oxygen from the iron oxide in the ore. Zinc is extracted by oxygen replacing sulphur in the zinc sulphide ore and the zinc oxide that is formed reacting with carbon in the coke to form carbon monoxide and zinc metal.

The temperature of the blast furnace in which iron is extracted is above the metal's melting point but below its boiling point, and the iron leaves the furnace as a liquid.

# EARTH MATERIALS

The temperature of the blast furnace in which zinc is extracted is above the metal's boiling point and it leaves the furnace as a vapour.

**19** It forms a layer of zinc oxide on its surface which prevents further reaction with oxygen in the air. Iron rusts in air when the metal is wet.

## Aluminium (PB page 132)

**20** Because it can be used in a wide variety of ways such as for wrapping foods and for making pans that are easy to lift, aircraft, vans, racing bicycles and metal fittings on ships.

**21** oxygen

## Carbon (PB pages 134 and 135)

**22** It has more clay because graphite is a soft material and clay is harder.

**23** Both are formed in igneous rock but graphite also forms in metamorphic rock. Both can be made artificially by heating but diamonds are made at a lower temperature but at a higher pressure.

The carbon atoms in graphite form hexagonal structures. In diamond they form tetrahedral structures. The hexagonal structures are held together by weak forces. The tetrahedral structures are held together by strong forces.

Graphite is used to make pencils and lubricants. Diamonds are used to make drills and jewellery.

Graphite and most diamonds are dark and opaque but some diamonds are transparent.

**24** This statement is true. Carbon as graphite is used to make pencils for drawing and lubricants to make machinery run smoothly. Carbon as diamond is used to make drills to search for oil or to cut through concrete, glass and metals. Carbon as charcoal is used as a barbecue fuel where it provides heat without smoke, and in gas masks and aquarium filters where it removes harmful substances from the air and water respectively. Carbon as coke is used to extract some metals. It is alloyed with iron to make steel.

## Sulphur (PB page 137)

**25**

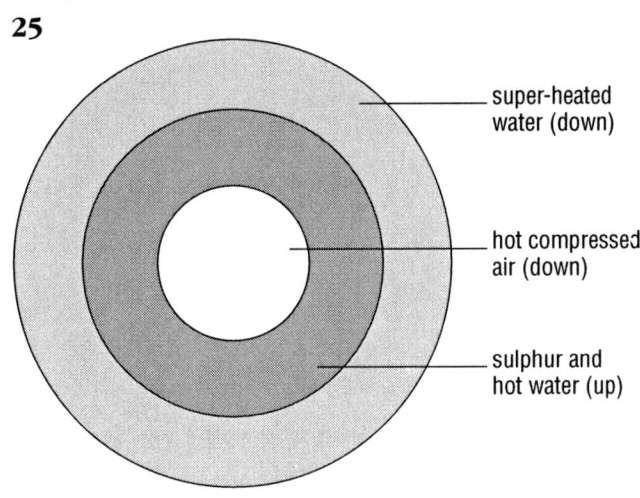

## End of chapter question (PB page 138)

**1** See opposite.

## End of chapter test (WORKSHEET 10.2, TRB page 73)

**1** a mixture of metals or of a metal and a non-metal, such as iron and carbon to make steel

**2 a)** Because aluminium is much more reactive than gold, which is a very unreactive metal.
   **b)** native elements

**3 a)** iron  **b)** aluminium  **c)** lead
   **d)** zinc  **e)** copper

**4 a)** carbon
   **b)** carbon dioxide and carbon monoxide
   **c)** carbon monoxide
   **d)** carbon monoxide + iron oxide
      → iron + carbon dioxide

**5 a)** calcium carbonate
      → calcium oxide + carbon dioxide
   **b)** calcium oxide
   **c)** impurities in the haematite
   **d)** calcium silicate

**6** By blowing oxygen through it to reduce the amount of carbon in the mixture.

**7 a)** steel  **b)** gold  **c)** lead  **d)** aluminium
   **e)** silver  **f)** zinc  **g)** cast iron  **h)** copper

**8 a)** diamond, graphite, buckminsterfullerene
   **b) i)** diamond  **ii)** graphite  **iii)** diamond
      **iv)** graphite

**9** making sulphuric acid, rubber, fungicide

## ANSWERS

This table shows examples of what could be included in the answer to the End of chapter question (PB page 138).

| Substance | Sources | Extraction | Properties | Uses |
|---|---|---|---|---|
| gold | hydrothermal vents, rocky particles in streams and river beds | panning, mining, dissolving in potassium cyanide, filtering, a precipitation reaction | does not react with air, keeps a shiny appearance, soft and easily shaped, conducts electricity, does not corrode | jewellery, decoration of buildings and books, electrical contacts |
| silver | hydrothermal vents on its own or as silver glance (silver sulphide), recycled metals | in electrolysis as copper, zinc and lead are being purified | high reflectivity, soft, tarnishes in air | jewellery, cutlery, ornaments, coins, in photographic industry |
| copper | copper pyrites | concentration in flotation cell; roasted in furnace, electrolysis | soft, does not react with water, conducts heat and electricity well, corrodes slowly | water pipes, electrical wiring, kitchen pans |
| lead | galena (lead sulphide) | concentration in flotation cell, roasted in furnace, electrolysis | easily shaped, does not corrode, prevents passage of harmful radiation | flashing on roofs, car batteries, handling of radioactive materials |
| iron | haematite (iron oxide) | blast furnace with coke and limestone | can be cast into moulds | manhole covers in streets, car engine blocks |
| steel | iron from blast furnace | not extracted, but made by heating iron in oxygen to remove some of the carbon | rusts, can be made into magnets | wide range of uses, e.g. car bodies, paperclips, girders |
| zinc | zinc blende (zinc sulphide) | concentration in flotation cell, roasted in a furnace, heated in a blast furnace | forms an oxide layer which prevents corrosion, easily shaped | electrical cells, flashing, coating steel to prevent corrosion |
| aluminium | bauxite (aluminium hydroxide) | converted to aluminium oxide by treatment with sodium hydroxide, electrolysis of aluminium oxide | soft, weak, lightweight, non-toxic, good electrical conductor | food wrapping, overhead power cables, kitchen pans, aircraft, vans, racing bicycles |
| carbon (graphite) | pure form in igneous and metamorphic rocks, can be made artificially | mining | soft and opaque | pencils and lubricants |
| carbon (diamond) | pure form in igneous rocks, can be made artificially | mining | very hard, most opaque but some transparent | drills and jewellery |
| carbon (charcoal) | wood | heating wood in absence of air | absorbs gases | barbecue fuel, gas masks and water filters |
| carbon (coke) | coal | heating coal in absence of air | reducing agent | extraction of iron, zinc and lead |
| sulphur | some sedimentary rocks like limestone | super-heated water and compressed air | brittle yellow solid, poisonous to fungi | making sulphuric acid, fungicide, vulcanisation of rubber |

# EARTH MATERIALS

## IT input

Hall of Fame:

- Benin bronze, PB page 124
- Hittites, PB page 128
- Herman Frasch, PB page 136

As an alternative to the End of chapter question on page 138, you could instruct pupils to use your school's database program to create a database and interrogate it. (There will be a *record* for each element and a number of *fields* for each of the characteristics. Fields for properties could be increased to make more sophisticated searches of the database: examples might include colour, hardness, toxicity and strength. The database could then be asked for a list of elements that are soft, silver metals, or are yellow and toxic, or whose names begin with the letter 's'. More enthusiastic pupils may be encouraged to extend the list of elements beyond those required by the questions, or to add extra fields.)

## Activities

### Activity 10.1 Panning for 'gold'

*Gold* (PB page 121)

This activity may be used with younger pupils at the beginning of their course when they are studying the separation of substances. Demonstrate the swirling action needed to lift the sand and water out of the dish, then let the pupils try. Ask them to compare the technique with other methods of separation and look for words such as 'sediment' and 'decanting' in their answers.

**Preparation**
- For each class group: beaker of sand with small brass turnings mixed into it, shallow dish, large bowl of water

**Safety**
- Eye protection must be worn.

### Activity 10.2 Comparing minerals

*Metals* (PB page 120)

This activity could also be done following Activity 8.4 (TRB page 55).

Present the pupils with a selection of ores and ask them to work out an identification scheme. Introduce the streak test with an unglazed white tile. When some minerals are rubbed on the tile they leave a characteristic coloured streak which can be used for identification purposes, for example iron pyrites (iron sulphide) has a greenish black streak while haematite (iron oxide) has a red or red-brown streak. In the comparison look for descriptions featuring colour, crystal shape, streak and weight. Some pupils may also try the hardness test if they have already done Activity 8.4. The hardness of the minerals is given in brackets under 'Preparation' below.

Extend by introducing bauxite and see whether the pupils can correctly suggest that it is made from several minerals. (These are diaspore, AlO(OH), which is translucent white, pink, brown or grey, gibbsite, $Al(OH)_3$, which is transparent or translucent and white, red or pink, boehmite, AlO(OH), in tiny crystals, and oxides of iron.)

**Preparation**
- For each class group: samples of silver glance (2½), chalcopyrite (3½), galena (2½), haematite (5–6) and sphalerite (4)

**Safety**
- Eye protection must be worn.

### Activity 10.3 Making a plastic substance

*Plastics and metals* (PB page 132)

WORKSHEET 10.1 Making casein (TRB page 72)
Issue the worksheet and ask the pupils to make casein – a plastic made from milk.

The activity can be extended by investigating the action of heat on the hardening of the plastic. (If the lumps are kept warm they harden faster.) Casein is used to make buttons, buckles and napkin rings but more chemicals are used in the hardening process.

## Preparation
- For each class group: beaker, tripod, gauze, Bunsen burner, heatproof mat, milk, measuring cylinder, vinegar, glass rod, jar, muslin, elastic band
- For the extension: a warm cupboard

**Safety**
- Eye protection must be worn.
- Pupils must be warned not to taste the milk because of the contamination risk.
- Make sure that the tripods have cooled down before clearing them away.

# Activity 10.4 Reducing with carbon

*Coke* (PB page 135)

Let the pupils mix a small quantity of a charcoal/carbon mixture with an equal quantity of copper oxide and heat the mixture in an ignition tube. The tube should be heated strongly until the mixture glows, then it should be allowed to cool. The pupils should look for a thin pink layer of copper in the tube.

This activity may be used as an example of reduction to supplement those in Chapter 5.

## Preparation
- For each class group: ignition tube, test-tube holder, test-tube rack, Bunsen burner, heatproof mat
- Chemicals: charcoal/carbon mixture, copper oxide

**Safety**
- Eye protection must be worn.

EARTH MATERIALS

# WORKSHEET 10.1 *Making casein*

 Eye protection must be worn

! Do not taste the milk

! Make sure that the tripod has cooled down before clearing it away

1. Measure out 250 cm³ of milk into a beaker.
2. Warm the milk but do not let it boil.
3. Add 10 cm³ of vinegar and stir it into the milk.
4. Leave the mixture to cool.
5. Fasten a piece of muslin over a jar with an elastic band.
6. Pour the mixture slowly onto the muslin.
7. Press the solid lumps of plastic together to form a flat slab of plastic.
8. Note the properties of the plastic, then leave it for a few days and examine its properties again.
9. Record your observations in a table below.

# WORKSHEET 10.2 *End of chapter test*

1. What is an alloy?
2. **a)** Why is gold found on its own but aluminium is found combined with other elements?
   **b)** What is the name given to elements that are found on their own in the Earth's crust?
3. Which metal is extracted from **a)** haematite, **b)** bauxite, **c)** galena, **d)** sphalerite, **e)** chalcopyrite?
4. **a)** What is the element in coke which takes part in a chemical reaction with oxygen in the blast furnace?
   **b)** Which gases does this element form in the blast furnace?
   **c)** Which gas reacts with iron oxide in the ore?
   **d)** Construct a word equation for the reaction between the gas and iron oxide.
5. **a)** Construct the word equation to describe the reaction which occurs when limestone is heated in the blast furnace.
   **b)** Which of the products in this reaction reacts with silicon oxide?
   **c)** What is the source of silicon oxide in the blast furnace?
   **d)** What is the chemical name for slag?
6. How is iron converted into steel?
7. Which metal in the list below is used for **a)** girders, **b)** decorating books, **c)** X-ray protection, **d)** food wrapping, **e)** photography, **f)** galvanisation, **g)** car engine blocks, **h)** electrical wiring?

   gold    silver    steel    zinc    cast iron    aluminium    copper    lead

8. **a)** What are the three forms of pure carbon?
   **b)** Which form is used for making **i)** drills, **ii)** lubricants, **iii)** jewellery, **iv)** pencil leads?
9. Name three uses of sulphur.

# 11 The chemical industry

## Answers

### The chemical industry (PB page 139)

1. inks, dyes, fibres such as nylon, medicines, processed foods, washing powders, oven cleaners, nail varnish, cosmetics, paper, fertilisers, rubber, metals
2. If the total cost of the raw materials, energy used and expenses in building and running the plant are higher than the money received for selling the product, a loss would be made.

### Women chemical engineers (PB page 140)

1. In the batch process a certain amount of a chemical is made at one time. In the continuous process the product is made continuously and a larger amount of product can be made in a certain time.
2. They design and operate chemical plants.
3. At first there were only men chemical engineers but by 1990 two thirds of the new graduate chemical engineers were men and one third were women, so there is a larger proportion of women chemical engineers now than in the past.

### Sulphuric acid (PB pages 141 and 142)

3. It is melted and sprayed into a furnace containing dry air.
4. The pressure would allow the reactants to come closer together to increase the rate of reaction, and more reactants could be held in that part of the plant than if the reactants were not under pressure.
5. It speeded up the reaction.
6. In stage 3 – the sulphur trioxide is dissolved in sulphuric acid to make oleum and water is added to the oleum to dilute it and produce sulphuric acid.

**For discussion** Fibres are used in the clothes of the people involved in the production of the tin of soup – the farmer, steelworkers, workers at the food processing factory, the van driver. Soap is used by the farmer for personal hygiene after harvesting the vegetables and by the food factory workers before and after work. Insecticide is sprayed on the crop so there are no losses due to insects eating the vegetables.

### Sodium hydroxide (PB pages 142 and 143)

7. brine
8. It is used in making soap for cleaning the skin, in oven cleaners for removing grease and in bleach for killing germs.
9. in processing the paper
10. Hydrogen is made by the electrolysis of brine. It is used as a fuel in the rocket motor to provide the thrust to take the rocket into space.

### Ammonia (PB page 144)

11. nitrogen and hydrogen
12. Very important, because if he had not changed it the original metal could have broken, with disastrous results and loss of production.
13. To make sure more ammonia is produced than is changed back into hydrogen and nitrogen.
14. fertiliser

### Nitric acid (PB page 145)

15. ammonia and air
16. It is used to make explosives such as TNT.

### The petrochemical industry (PB page 147)

17. a) D, B, E, A, C
    b) D – refinery gas, used as a fuel;
       B – gasoline, used as a fuel in cars;
       E – naphtha, used to make chemicals;
       A – kerosene, used as a fuel in jet engines;
       C – diesel oil or gas oil, used as a fuel in diesel engines
    c) The fractions with higher boiling points contain longer chain molecules.
18. Gases move up through the risers and out under the bubble caps, then escape from the liquid and move up to the next set of risers.
19. Liquids move down through overflow pipes.

20 gasoline, kerosene, diesel oil, lubricating oil, fuel oil and residue
21 Because more short chain molecules are needed than long chain molecules.

## Finding a site for an industrial plant (PB page 148)

**For discussion** A range of options may be considered. For example, it may be considered best to site the plant close to town 2 (on the same side of the river), bring materials B and C to the head of the river, widen it and transport them to the plant. Alternatively, site the plant on the opposite bank, bring B and C by rail and build a bridge to link the town and the plant, the finished material leaving by sea. Another option would be to widen the mouth of the river on the right to make a harbour, put in a smaller bridge to link the town and the plant on the opposite shore, and bring B and C to the plant by railway and send the product on a railway through a gap in the hills.

## End of chapter question (PB page 149)

1 heating – to produce combustion, to provide energy for chemical reactions to take place, to melt solid materials and to boil liquid materials
dissolving – e.g. gases in liquids, such as sulphur trioxide being dissolved in sulphuric acid
electrolysis – to split up raw materials into elements, for the formation of compounds such as sodium hydroxide
use of pressure – to increase the concentration, to prevent reactions from reversing
use of catalyst – to speed up reactions
fractional distillation – for separation of substances in petroleum

## End of chapter test (WORKSHEET 11.1, TRB page 77)

1 a substance that is used at the beginning of a process to make new materials
2 **a)** iron ore (haematite), coke and limestone
  **b)** sulphur, oxygen and water
3 **a)** a synthesis reaction
  **b)** The reaction is reversible.

**c) i)** The gas molecules are pushed closer together so they can react more quickly, and more materials can be pressed into a space in the industrial plant.
  **ii)** Chemical reactions take place faster at higher temperatures.
  **iii)** The catalyst increases the rate of the reaction.
4 fertilisers, detergents, battery acid, extraction of titanium, making fibres, soap and insecticides
5 brine
6 chemicals, synthetic fibres, soap, oven cleaners, bleach, dyes, pharmaceuticals, extraction of aluminium, processing of wood
7 **a)** air (nitrogen) and natural gas (hydrogen)
  **b)** the Haber process
8 fertilisers, oven cleaners, dry cells, nitric acid
9 from dead bodies of tiny animals and plants that lived in the seas over 200 million years ago
10 fractional distillation
11 **a) i)** B  **ii)** C
   **b)**

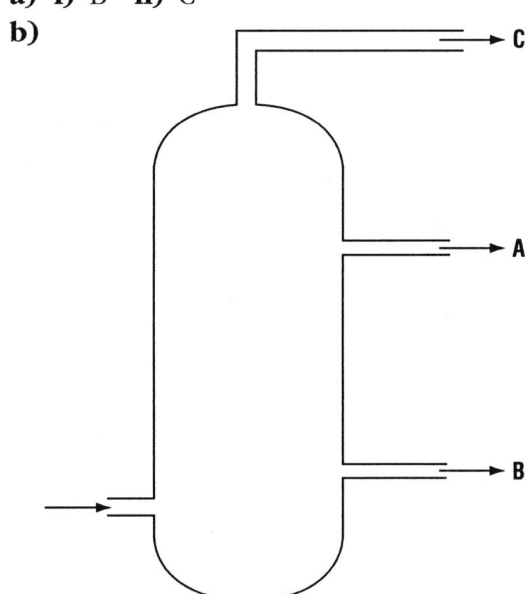

   **c) i)** A and B
     **ii)** The long chain molecules are broken into smaller ones.
     **iii)** There is a greater demand for short chain molecules than for long chain molecules to make the materials we need.

## IT input

Hall of Fame:

- Fritz Haber, PB page 144
- Karl Bosch, PB page 144

# THE CHEMICAL INDUSTRY

## Activities

### Activity 11.1 Product survey

*The chemical industry* (PB page 139)

This activity can be used with younger pupils as an introduction to the chapter. Ask the pupils to look at the labels of empty shampoo, bath creme, soap and toothpaste containers and note any elements or compounds that they recognise.

The activity can be extended by looking at the chemicals in packaged foods such as packet soups.

#### Preparation

- Empty shampoo, bath creme, soap and toothpaste containers, cleaned out thoroughly but with their labels still intact
- Containers of packaged foods, e.g. packet soup

### Activity 11.2 Investigating washing powders

*The chemical industry* (PB page 139)

Ask the pupils to devise a way of comparing the effectiveness of a biological washing powder and a non-biological powder at removing a stain such as egg yolk on cloth. Pupils' plans must be checked by a teacher before the practical work begins.

#### Preparation

- For each class group: measuring cylinder, beaker, glass rod, spatulas, thermometer, tripod, gauze, Bunsen burner, heatproof mat, protective gloves
- Top pan balance
- Biological and non-biological washing powders, cloths, runny egg yolk or other suitable stain from a biological source (e.g. gravy)

#### Safety

- Eye protection must be worn.
- Some biological powders may produce an allergic response in some pupils. Ensure that they wear protective gloves.
- Make sure that the tripods have cooled down before clearing them away.

# WORKSHEET 11.1 *End of chapter test*

1. What is a raw material?
2. What are the raw materials from which **a)** iron, **b)** sulphuric acid are made?
3. This is one of the reactions which takes place in the production of sulphuric acid:

    sulphur dioxide + oxygen ⇌ sulphur trioxide

    **a)** Is the reaction **i)** a synthesis reaction, **ii)** a neutralisation reaction, or **iii)** a precipitation reaction?
    **b)** What does the symbol ⇌ tell you about the reaction?
    **c)** How do the following help in the production of sulphuric acid?
      **i)** The pressure of the reactants is twice atmospheric pressure.
      **ii)** The gases are heated to 400–500°C.
      **iii)** The gases pass over a catalyst.
4. Name three uses of sulphuric acid.
5. What is the raw material from which sodium hydroxide is made?
6. Name three uses of sodium hydroxide.
7. **a)** What are the raw materials for making ammonia?
    **b)** What is the name of the process by which ammonia is made industrially?
8. Name three uses of ammonia.
9. From what have oil and natural gas formed?
10. What is the process used to separate the different hydrocarbons in oil?
11. The table shows the chain length of three groups of hydrocarbons in oil.

| Group | Carbon atoms in molecule |
|---|---|
| A | 10–16 |
| B | 20–50 |
| C | 1–4 |

**a)** Which group has **i)** the highest boiling point, **ii)** the lowest boiling point?
**b)** Mark on the tower the pipes you would expect to collect A, B and C.

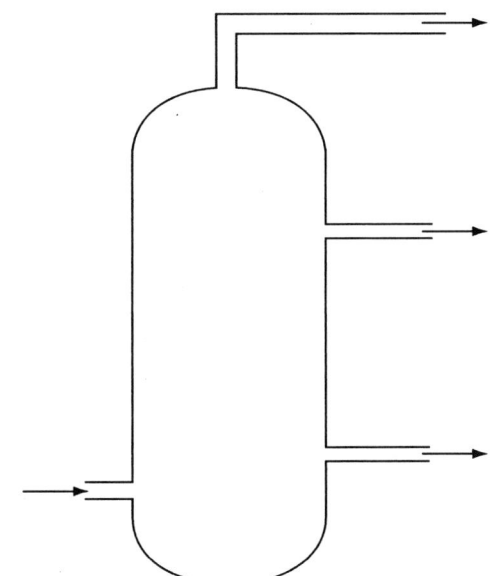

**c) i)** Which groups take part in a process called cracking, **ii)** what happens in this process, and **iii)** why is it used?

# 12 Chemicals and the environment

# Answers

## Chemicals and the environment

(PB pages 151 and 152)

1. stone, wood, animal skin, bones, antlers, shells
2. The human population was small and as materials had to be made by hand they were produced in small quantities. Any wastes that caused pollution were also produced in small quantities.
3. The air and water would dilute the wastes and make them harmless.

**For discussion** Having a simpler life style would reduce all kinds of environmental damage, but the size of the human population is too large for this to be realistic using the technology we have today. For example, food production and storage need industrial processes to provide a steady supply of food for all the people living today. A simpler life style would need a smaller human population, and a long-term project to reduce the size of the human population would be difficult as in the developed countries people are living longer and this would mean that fewer people would be able to have children.

## The Earth's changing atmosphere

(PB page 153)

1. The first atmosphere was composed of carbon dioxide, water vapour, ammonia and methane. Later, oxygen was produced by plants, and it reacted with ammonia to produce nitrogen. There is a layer of ozone which is now getting smaller.
2. plants and bacteria, use of CFCs
3. Life as we have it on Earth now has not evolved on Venus or Mars.

**For discussion** It is leading to more people suffering from skin cancers. A tanned skin has in the past been thought to be healthy but people should not sunbathe now, to reduce their chance of developing skin cancers. People who go out in the sun should wear a sunscreen lotion or only stay in the sun for a short time.

## Air pollution (PB pages 153—157)

**For discussion** A wide ranging discussion could include the following topics. Initially we would not be able to use most electrical devices, which would have to be adapted to run on batteries that could be recharged by small wind turbines and water wheels. In time, some devices may be developed to run on clockwork, like the clockwork radio now in use in parts of Africa. All timing devices would have to be clockwork. Heat and light could be provided by gas or oil. Steam power may return to industry and to trains.

4. They are opaque, so when they settle on leaves they prevent light reaching the leaf cells and prevent photosynthesis taking place.
5. It combines with haemoglobin in the blood and stops the haemoglobin carrying oxygen to the cells.
6. a) The plants by the lake may be contaminated with soot. Acid rain may affect the water and cause the fish and other forms of water life to die.
   b) Global warming may occur in which the polar ice melts and the sea level rises, perhaps causing the sea to flood into the lake.
7. a) The concentration of the acids in the snow increases as the water evaporates.
   b) i)

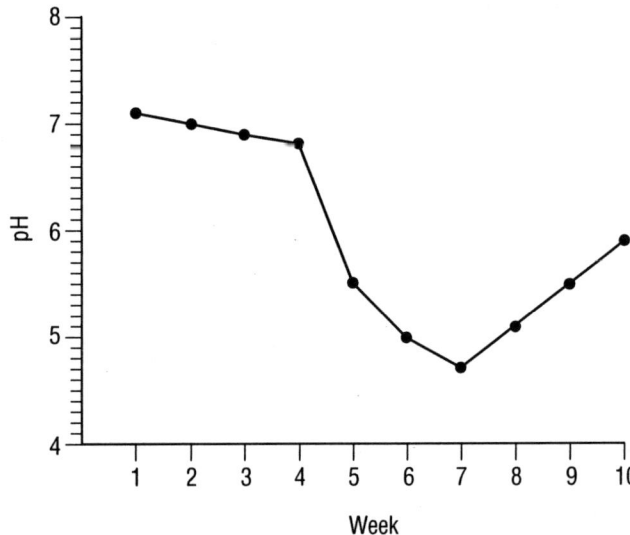

ii) The snow from which water had previously evaporated has now melted and caused the pH of the river to fall.

# ANSWERS

**iii)** As it is warmer the snow is melting more quickly and there is less time for evaporation.

**iv)** It will continue to rise. It will be too warm for ice to form and rain will fall. This will have a lower concentration of acid than the ice.

## Improving air quality
(PB pages 157—159)

**8** It solves the problem of air pollution locally and causes dilution of the pollutants, but it does not destroy them so it does not completely solve the problem of air pollution.

**9 a)** The price of the product is increased if money has to be spent on treating the waste gases.

**b)** The company could sell the substances it produces as it cleans the waste gases. The money received from these substances could be used to reduce the price of the product.

**10** The honeycomb structure provides a very large surface area for chemical reactions to take place.

**For discussion** Use electricity more sparingly, for example switching lights off in rooms that are not being used, to reduce power station output. Use cars which run on unleaded petrol and have catalytic converters. Use the cars less frequently by sharing trips or using public transport which can move large numbers of people with less pollution. People running factories should ensure that the wastes produced are converted into useful substances.

## Water pollution (PB pages 159 and 160)

**11** Heavy metals in the water can cause cancer. PCBs and mercury pass into food chains and can cause permanent damage and death if living things in the river are used for food.

**12** They ate fish which contained large amounts of mercury that had passed up the food chain and become concentrated in the fishes' bodies.

**13** The oil reduces the amount of oxygen entering the sea water that can be used for respiration and reduces the amount of light entering the water that can be used for photosynthesis.

## Chemicals and the land environment
(PB page 162)

**14** Open cast mining destroys the habitat. In rainforests it also causes soil erosion which prevents the habitat re-forming when the mining has finished. Sinking mine shafts causes little damage but some damage will be done by making roads and living quarters for the miners.

## Renewable and non-renewable materials (PB page 163)

**15 a)** In planted forests there are few tree species and the trees are all the same age and regularly spaced out. In natural forests there are more tree species and the trees are different ages and irregularly spaced out.

**b)** The natural forests will support more wildlife as the greater number of tree species and wider range of ages will offer a wider variety of food (also setting up more food chains) and provide a wider variety of places where animals can make nests or hide away.

**16 a)** 40 years

**b)** This will depend on the year this work is studied.

## Recycling (PB page 164)

**17 a)** 35.7 years

**b)** This will depend on the year this work is studied.

**18 a) i)** 200 years  **ii)** 125 years

**b)** It makes the reserves of the material last 160 years longer, or 89.3 years longer if the new product is produced.

**19** This will depend on the year this work is studied.

**20** It saves space, energy and raw materials.

## Materials and energy (PB page 165)

**21** No – they will not last so long, as the coal will be used to replace gas and oil.

**22** It makes the stocks of fossil fuels last longer because less energy is used in recycling than in extraction.

# CHEMICALS AND THE ENVIRONMENT

## End of chapter question (PB page 166)

1 All factories and industrial plants should prevent air pollution by having precipitators on their chimneys and should treat waste gases with chemicals to make useful products. Waste materials should not be discharged into rivers but be recycled. Industries should use heat energy as efficiently as possible to reduce the use of fuel. Better public transport systems should be set up.

Tips should be used as a source of methane. More vehicles should run on unleaded petrol. All vehicles should have catalytic converters. Forestry programmes should use a wider range of tree species and allow for trees to be irregularly spaced and to be cut down at different ages.

## End of chapter test (WORKSHEET 12.1, TRB page 82)

1 a) carbon dioxide  b) sulphur dioxide
   c) carbon monoxide
2 The acid rain dissolves some of the minerals and carries them away. The plants cannot grow properly without minerals.
3 a) i) snail, mayfly, grayling, perch and eel
      ii) grayling, perch and eel  iii) eel
      iv) none of them
   b) The lower the pH, the fewer water animals can survive.
4 a) smoke and water droplets in the air
   b) It damages the lining of the respiratory system.
5 a) to improve combustion
   b) It forms particles in the air which can be taken into the body and which damage the nervous system including the brain.
6 a) It protects living things from harmful ultraviolet rays from the Sun.
   b) CFCs (chlorofluorocarbons)
   c) aerosols and refrigerators
   d) carbon dioxide and hydrocarbon gases
7 PCBs (polychlorinated biphenyls), heavy metals (cadmium, chromium, nickel and lead), mercury, detergents, oil
8 They can cause cancers.
9 Wood is renewable because when trees have been chopped down for their timber new trees can be planted and grown to replace them. Coal is not renewable because it is not replaced when it is used up.
10 It reduces the rate at which the reserves of coal are being used up, so more is conserved for the future. Less coal is needed for melting the iron and recycling it than for providing coke for extracting the metal from its ore.

## IT input

Pupils can use CD-ROMs and the Internet to search for information on CFCs, acid rain and PCBs.

# Activities

## Activity 12.1  Wind and acid rain

### Acid rain makers (PB page 155)

This investigation is a long-term project. The pupils collect rain from the school rain gauge and test its pH. They also note the direction of the prevailing wind during the time that the rain was collected. Over a period of months a wind rose can be produced showing the pH of the rain. Any close association between wind direction and pH can be investigated by looking at maps for a possible source of the acid rain.

An alternative or introductory activity would be to have the pupils test up to 20 samples of 'rainwater' which have been given wind direction data and allow them to test them and build up a wind rose straight away.

### Preparation
- For each class group: pH indicator paper, test-tubes
- A rain gauge and wind vane set up in the school weather station
- For the alternative/introductory activity: 20 samples of water with a range of pH values from 7 to 2, with the more acidic samples associated with a particular wind direction (perhaps south, south-west or west)

### Safety
- Eye protection must be worn for the alternative/introductory activity.

## Activity 12.2 How dirty is the rain?

*Improving air quality* (PB page 157)

A white-painted surface can be exposed to the rain for a certain time, perhaps half an hour, then brought inside and allowed to dry. The surface can be examined with a hand lens or binocular microscope for signs of solid pollutants.

**Preparation**
- For each class group: a square of white-painted board with a side length of at least 10 cm, hand lens
- One or more binocular microscopes

## Activity 12.3 Recycling survey

*Recycling* (PB page 164)

Ask the pupils to conduct a survey to find out how many families in the class recycle paper, cans, glass and clothes. (This could be extended to include other environmentally helpful activities such as using unleaded petrol and public transport.)

## Activity 12.4 Investigating fertilisers in water

*Water pollution* (PB page 159)

Ask the pupils to devise an investigation to test the effect of fertiliser on pond water. In their plan look for the use of three or more samples of pond water – one sample with no fertiliser added and the other samples with increasing amounts added. Look also for criteria for comparing the samples, e.g. greenness of the water due to algae, the regular checking of samples over the coming weeks and topping up the water to match losses due to evaporation. When the plans have been checked allow the pupils to set up their investigation.

**Preparation**
- For each class group: jars, chinagraph pencil
- For the class: pond water from an unpolluted source (or water collected from flower vases), fertiliser, e.g. Baby bio

**Safety**
- Eye protection must be worn.
- Beware of the risk of Weil's disease from contaminated pond water. All cuts should be covered with waterproof plasters.

CHEMICALS AND THE ENVIRONMENT

# WORKSHEET 12.1  *End of chapter test*

1. Which gas from the list below:
   a) contributes greatly to global warming,
   b) contributes greatly to acid rain,
   c) reacts with haemoglobin in the blood?

         carbon monoxide    carbon dioxide    sulphur dioxide

2. Why do plants become stunted and die in regions which receive acid rain?
3. The table shows the minimum pH of water at which certain water animals can survive.

   | Animal | Minimum pH |
   | --- | --- |
   | eel | 4.5 |
   | perch | 5 |
   | grayling | 5.5 |
   | mayfly | 5.75 |
   | snail | 6 |

   a) Which of these animals would you expect to find in water with a pH of **i)** 6.5, **ii)** 5.6, **iii)** 4.8, **iv)** 4?
   b) What pattern can you see in your answers to part **a)**?
4. a) What is smog, and b) how is it harmful?
5. a) Why was lead added to petrol?
   b) How is lead in petrol harmful?
6. a) Why is the ozone layer important to life on Earth?
   b) Which chemicals are destroying the ozone layer?
   c) From which manufactured products did these chemicals escape?
   d) What replacements are now being used for these chemicals?
7. Name five substances from industry that pollute water.
8. How can radioactive materials harm the human body?
9. Wood is a renewable material but coal is a non-renewable material. Why are they described in this way?
10. How does increasing the recycling of iron affect the reserves of coal in the ground? Explain your answer.

# 13 The periodic table

# Answers

## Sorting out the elements (PB page 168)

1 It led to the idea of atomic weights.
2 They saw that when the elements were set out in order of their atomic weights the properties of the elements varied periodically.
3 The new elements fitted into the gaps that Mendeleev had left in his table.

## Groups of the periodic table
(PB pages 170—173)

1 a) increases  b) decreases  c) decreases
2 potassium – it has a lower density than sodium
3 They will be softer.
4 caesium
5 a) below sodium  b) above potassium
6 a) increases  b) decreases  c) decreases

**For discussion** The trends are less well established in the alkaline earth metals than in the alkali metals.

7 The melting points and boiling points rise as you go down the group.
8 a) astatine and iodine – the melting points are well above room temperature of about 20°C
   b) bromine – the melting point is below room temperature but the boiling point is above room temperature
   c) chlorine and fluorine – the boiling points are below room temperature
9 No – the alkali metals and alkaline earth metals are more reactive towards the bottom of the table. This is because potassium is higher than sodium in the reactivity series and calcium is higher than magnesium in the reactivity series.

## End of chapter question (PB page 175)

1 These elements are important in our lives. For example, sodium and potassium are used in sending impulses along our nerves and potassium is used for controlling the water content of the body. Potassium is also used to make fertiliser for growing plants while sodium is used to make sodium hydroxide and sodium carbonate, which have a wide range of uses. Sodium is also used in street lights and alloyed with potassium for use in nuclear reactors which make electricity. Lithium is used to make batteries and as a medicine to treat mental disorders. Rubidium and caesium are used in photoelectric cells.

Magnesium is used by plants to make chlorophyll which is essential for photosynthesis, and in our bodies it is used to make teeth and bones. It is used in alloys to make lightweight metals. Calcium is used in the body to make bones and teeth and for the contraction of muscles. It is used in a wide range of products from baking powder to plastic. Strontium is used in flares to help locate survivors of shipwrecks. Barium is used in the making of X-ray photographs of the alimentary canal. Beryllium is used in nuclear reactors which make electricity.

Iodine is used to produce a hormone in the body and as an antiseptic. Chlorine is used to kill bacteria and in the making of hydrochloric acid which is widely used in the chemical industry. Bromine and iodine are used in photography and fluorine is used to prevent tooth decay.

## End of chapter test (WORKSHEET 13.2, TRB page 86)

1 relative atomic mass
2 It tells you how many protons are in the nucleus.
3 a) sodium, potassium and lithium
   b) calcium, magnesium and barium
   c) chlorine, fluorine and iodine
4 They increase.
5 They increase.
6 a) sodium  b) beryllium  c) calcium
   d) strontium  e) bromine
7 calcium and chlorine
8 Dalton
9 Mendeleev

# THE PERIODIC TABLE

**10 a), b)**

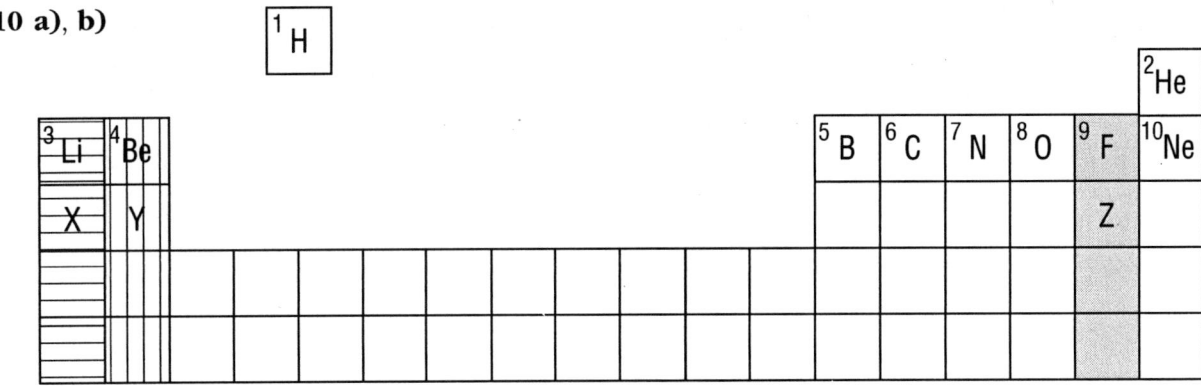

c) X sodium, Y magnesium, Z chlorine

## IT input

Hall of Fame:

- John Dalton, PB page 167
- John Newlands, PB page 168
- Dmitri Mendeleev, PB page 168

CD-ROMs: there are several CD-ROMs dealing with the periodic table. These vary in approach and usefulness, but the best of them are very good and are sure to enhance the pupils' interest and understanding. You should choose a title that is suitable for this age and ability level, and you should be familiar with its use.

## Activities

### Activity 13.1 Properties of the elements

*The periodic table* (PB page 168)

Details of this activity were given in Activity 9.1, when the properties of metals and non-metals were being studied. It may also be performed as a study of elemental properties.

**Safety**

- Eye protection must be worn.
- Sodium should be stored under oil as it is highly flammable.
- Sulphur is an irritant.
- Bromine is harmful if ingested.
- Mercury is toxic if ingested.

### Activity 13.2 Reaction with water

*The periodic table* (PB page 168)

Details of this activity were given in Activity 9.4. Most of the non-metals show no appreciable reaction with water, although a study of the oxides of the elements would be useful. The oxides of metals give alkaline solutions when reacted with water and the oxides of non-metals give acidic solutions (this has also been covered in Activity 9.2).

**Safety**

- Eye protection must be worn.
- Lithium, sodium and potassium are flammable, corrosive and cause burns. The alkaline solutions they produce with water are caustic.

### Activity 13.3 The reactivity of the halogens

*Group VII, the halogens* (PB page 173)

WORKSHEET 13.1 Reactivity of the halogens (TRB page 85)

The pupils will have learned that the most reactive element in the periodic table is fluorine. This experiment will enable them to complete a table recording the reactivities of the other halogens.

**Preparation**

- For each class group: test-tubes
- Chemicals: 1% chlorine water, 1% bromine water, 1% iodine water, sodium chloride solution, sodium bromide solution, sodium iodide solution

**Safety**

- Eye protection must be worn.
- Warn pupils to handle all solutions carefully.

THE PERIODIC TABLE

# WORKSHEET 13.1 *Reactivity of the halogens*

Eye protection must be worn

Handle all solutions with great care

1. Take three test-tubes and place about 5 cm³ of sodium chloride solution in each tube.
2. Add a few drops of bromine water to the first tube, a few drops of iodine solution to the second and a few drops of chlorine water to the third. Record your results in a table.
3. Repeat step 2 using sodium bromide solution in the test-tubes.
4. Repeat step 2 using sodium iodide solution in the test-tubes.

**Questions**

1. What does your table of results show?

2. Why does sodium chloride solution show no change on the addition of chlorine water? Is there a reaction occurring?

3. Explain why chlorine is the most reactive of the elements you have studied.

4. Explain why iodine is the least reactive of the elements you have studied.

© John Murray     *Chemistry Now! 11–14 Teacher's Resource Book*

THE PERIODIC TABLE

# WORKSHEET 13.2  *End of chapter test*

1. What does RAM stand for?
2. What does the atomic number tell you about the atoms of an element?
3. Which of the following elements are a) alkali metals, b) alkaline earth metals, c) halogens?

     chlorine   calcium   fluorine   sodium   magnesium
         lithium   potassium   iodine   barium

4. How do the densities of alkali metals and alkaline earth metals change as the atomic number of the elements increases?
5. How do the melting points of the halogens change as the atomic number of the elements increases?
6. Which element is a) used in certain kinds of street lamp, b) found in emerald, c) used in baking powder, d) used in survival flares, e) used in photographic film?
7. Which two elements are used in making bleach?
8. Who used atomic weights to compare elements?
9. Who devised the periodic table?
10.

| | | | | | | | | | | | | | | | | | |
|---|---|---|---|---|---|---|---|---|---|---|---|---|---|---|---|---|---|
| | | | H | | | | | | | | | | | | | | He |
| Li | Be | | | | | | | | | | | B | ⁶C | N | O | F | Ne |
| X | Y | | | | | | | | | | | | | | | Z | |
| | | | | | | | | | | | | | | | | | |

a) The atomic number of carbon is shown in the table. Fill in the atomic number of the other elements shown, excluding X, Y and Z.
b) Use horizontal lines to show the alkali metal group, vertical lines to show the alkaline earth metal group and shade in the halogen group.
c) What is the identity of X, Y and Z?

# 14 Using formulae

## Answers

### Using formulae (PB pages 176 and 177)

1. a) NaOH  b) $NaNO_3$  c) $Na_2SO_4$
2. a) $SO_2$  b) CO
3. It tells you how many atoms take part in the reaction and how they combine into groups.
4. a) $H_2 + I_2 \rightarrow 2HI$
   b) balanced
   c) $2K + 2H_2O \rightarrow 2KOH + H_2$
   d) $2Mg + O_2 \rightarrow 2MgO$
   e) $2KI \rightarrow 2K + I_2$
   f) balanced
   g) $2H_2O_2 \rightarrow 2H_2O + O_2$

### State symbols (PB page 178)

5. a) zinc oxide + hydrochloric acid $\rightarrow$ zinc chloride + water
   b), c), d) $ZnO(s) + 2HCl(aq) \rightarrow ZnCl_2(aq) + H_2O(l)$

### End of chapter question (PB page 178)

1. Equations might include the following (from PB pages 84, 70, 74 and 60):

   $CH_4(g) + 2O_2(g) \rightarrow CO_2(g) + 2H_2O(l)$
   $Zn(s) + 2HCl(aq) \rightarrow ZnCl_2(aq) + H_2(g)$
   $H_2SO_4(aq) + MgO(s) \rightarrow MgSO_4(aq) + H_2O(l)$
   $CaO(s) + H_2O(l) \rightarrow Ca(OH)_2(s)$

### End of chapter test (Worksheet 14.2, TRB page 89)

1. $CaCO_3(s) \rightarrow CaO(s) + CO_2(g)$
2. $CuCO_3(s) \rightarrow CuO(s) + CO_2(g)$
3. $2AgCl(s) \rightarrow 2Ag(s) + Cl_2(g)$
4. $2H_2O(l) \rightarrow 2H_2(g) + O_2(g)$
5. $CuO(s) + H_2(g) \rightarrow Cu(s) + H_2O(g)$
6. $AgNO_3(aq) + NaCl(s) \rightarrow AgCl(s) + NaNO_3(aq)$
7. $MgCO_3(s) + 2HCl(aq) \rightarrow MgCl_2(aq) + H_2O(l) + CO_2(g)$
8. $HNO_3(aq) + NaHCO_3(s) \rightarrow NaNO_3(aq) + H_2O(l) + CO_2(g)$

## IT input

Pupils can use CD-ROMs and the Internet to search for information on sodium chloride.

## Activities

### Activity 14.1 Calculating the formula of copper oxide

Worksheet 14.1 Calculating the formula of copper oxide (TRB page 88)
This activity is useful because it allows the pupils to calculate the formula of a compound for themselves. This topic, which many pupils find difficult, thus is no longer just a list of facts to be learned, but a practical investigation.

**Preparation**

- For each class group: copper coil, U-tube with cotton wool soaked in a 50/50 mixture of methanol and ethanol, glass tubing, test-tube with hole, Bunsen burner, heatproof mat
- Top pan balance
- Chemicals: copper oxide

**Safety**

- Eye protection must be worn.
- Copper oxide is harmful by ingestion.
- Methanol is toxic.
- Ethanol is highly flammable.

■ USING FORMULAE

# WORKSHEET 14.1 *Calculating the formula of copper oxide*

 Eye protection must be worn

 Copper oxide is harmful

 Handle methanol and ethanol with great care

1. Record the mass of the test-tube (A1). Add approximately 2 g of copper oxide and weigh the tube again (A2). Insert the copper coil into the tube and assemble the apparatus as shown below.

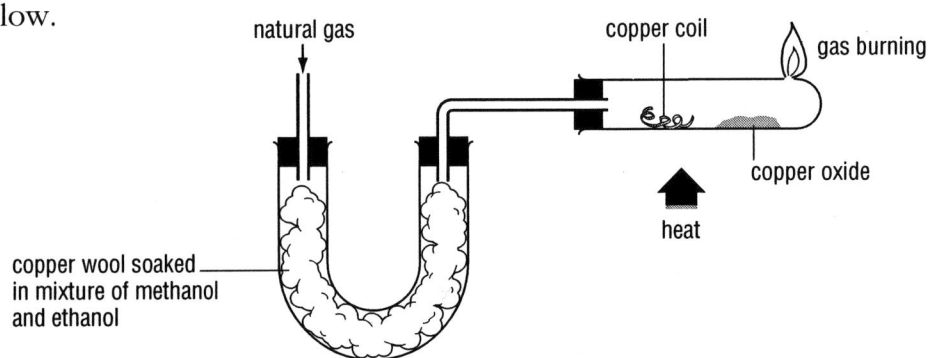

2. Connect the gas tap to the glass tubing so that natural gas is passed through the cotton wool. Allow the gas to pass over the apparatus for a few seconds to expel all the air before lighting the gas escaping through the small hole in the test-tube. Do not have the flame too large – adjust the gas so that a flame about 3 cm high is obtained.
3. Heat the test-tube evenly so that both the copper coil and the copper oxide are heated. Heat carefully at first, gradually increasing the heat until all the copper oxide has been reduced to copper (it should become brown).
4. Once the copper oxide has changed colour, remove the heat but continue to pass the gas over the apparatus until cool.
5. Once the apparatus is cold, dismantle the apparatus and remove the copper coil from the test-tube. Record the mass of the test-tube and the brown solid (A4).
6. Re-assemble the apparatus with a new piece of copper coil and repeat steps 2 to 5. When all the copper oxide has been reduced the mass of the test-tube will be constant.
7. Fill in your results below.

   Mass of test-tube = _____ g (A1)

   Mass of test-tube and copper oxide = _____ g (A2)

   Mass of copper oxide = A2 2 A1 = _____ g (A3)

   Final mass of test-tube and solid = _____ g (A4)

   Mass of copper = A4 2 A1 = _____ g (A5)

   Mass of oxygen combined with copper originally = A3 2 A5 = _____ g (A6)

A formula shows the ratio of the atoms in a compound. The ratio of copper atoms to oxygen atoms in copper oxide is found by dividing A5 by 63.5, the relative atomic mass of copper, to give A7, and dividing A6 by 16, the relative atomic mass of oxygen, to give A8.

We now have a ratio of atoms, A7 : A8. Dividing by the smaller number gives the simplest ratio. This will give the formula of copper oxide.

USING FORMULAE

# WORKSHEET 14.2 *End of chapter test*

Use these formulae to construct formula equations from the word equations below:

calcium Ca   carbon C   oxygen O   copper Cu   carbonate $CO_3$   chlorine Cl
nitrate $NO_3$   hydrochloric acid HCl   nitric acid $HNO_3$   hydrogencarbonate $HCO_3$

When you have completed each equation, put the state symbol for each element and compound in your equation.

1  calcium carbonate → calcium oxide + carbon dioxide
2  copper carbonate → copper oxide + carbon dioxide
3  silver chloride → silver + chlorine
4  water → hydrogen + oxygen
5  copper oxide + hydrogen → copper + water vapour
6  silver nitrate + sodium chloride → silver chloride + sodium nitrate
7  magnesium carbonate + hydrochloric acid → magnesium chloride + water + carbon dioxide
8  nitric acid + sodium hydrogencarbonate → sodium nitrate + water + carbon dioxide

---

# WORKSHEET 14.2 *End of chapter test*

Use these formulae to construct formula equations from the word equations below:

calcium Ca   carbon C   oxygen O   copper Cu   carbonate $CO_3$   chlorine Cl
nitrate $NO_3$   hydrochloric acid HCl   nitric acid $HNO_3$   hydrogencarbonate $HCO_3$

When you have completed each equation, put the state symbol for each element and compound in your equation.

1  calcium carbonate → calcium oxide + carbon dioxide
2  copper carbonate → copper oxide + carbon dioxide
3  silver chloride → silver + chlorine
4  water → hydrogen + oxygen
5  copper oxide + hydrogen → copper + water vapour
6  silver nitrate + sodium chloride → silver chloride + sodium nitrate
7  magnesium carbonate + hydrochloric acid → magnesium chloride + water + carbon dioxide
8  nitric acid + sodium hydrogencarbonate → sodium nitrate + water + carbon dioxide

© John Murray    Chemistry Now! 11–14 Teacher's Resource Book

# 13+ Question bank

1 Identify the pieces of apparatus in the diagrams.
   a)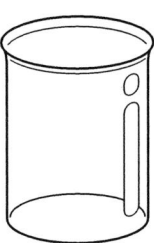
   b)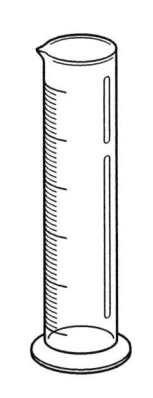
   c)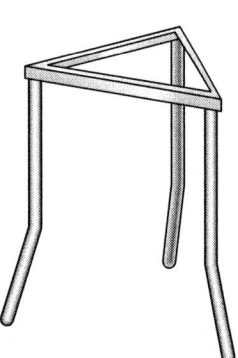

2 Make a diagram of **a)** a test-tube, **b)** a flat bottomed flask, **c)** a filter funnel.

3 **a)** Make a labelled diagram of a Bunsen burner.
   **b)** Put an X where the air and gas meet.
   **c)** Put a Y where a region of unburnt gas may form.

4 Describe each of the following processes with a word chosen from this list:

   freezing    condensing    evaporating
        boiling    melting    subliming

   **a)** the escape of gas bubbles from a hot liquid,
   **b)** the changing of a warm solid into a liquid,
   **c)** the changing of a cool gas into a liquid,
   **d)** the changing of a cool liquid into a solid.

5 Which diagram shows **a)** an atom, **b)** a molecule?

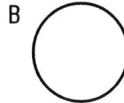

6 What are the elements present in **a)** magnesium oxide, **b)** iron sulphide?

7 Describe how you would separate sand and salt. Select some words from this list and use them in your answer:

   boiling    condensation    evaporation
   filtration    distillation    dissolve    solution

8 **a)** What kind of chemical reaction takes place when copper carbonate is heated?
   **b)** What are the products of this reaction?
   **c)** What are the forms of the products – solid, liquid or gas?

9 What are the reactants in a neutralisation reaction?

10 Three solutions, A, B and C, were tested with universal indicator paper. The paper in A went blue, the paper in B went red and the paper in C went green.
   **a)** Which solution has a pH of **i)** less than 7, **ii)** more than 7, **iii)** 7?
   **b)** Which solution is **i)** neutral, **ii)** an acid, **iii)** an alkali?

11 Which substance
   **a)** turns anhydrous copper sulphate powder from white to blue,
   **b)** turns lime water cloudy,
   **c)** re-lights a glowing splint that is plunged into a test-tube in which it has been collected,
   **d)** makes a squeaky pop when a flame is brought to the end of a test-tube in which it has been collected?

12 What is the density of a substance which has a mass of 8 g and a volume of 10 $cm^3$?

13 **a)** What are the reactants that take part in the rusting process?
   **b)** What is the chemical name for the product of this reaction?
   **c)** How can rusting be prevented?

**14 a)** What are the elements present in limestone?
  **b)** What happens to limestone when it is
    **i)** heated strongly, **ii)** treated with hydrochloric acid?

**15** Does a typical metal or a typical non-metal
  **a)** conduct electricity well, **b)** conduct heat poorly, **c)** have a shiny surface, **d)** form acidic oxides?

**16 a)** Magnesium, gold, copper and iron are four metals. Arrange them in order, starting with the most reactive and ending with the least reactive.
  **b) i)** Which of these four metals is found on its own? **ii)** Explain your answer.
  **c)** One of the metals produces bubbles of gas slowly when it is placed in water.
    **i)** Which metal is it? **ii)** What is the gas?
  **d) i)** Use a word equation to describe the reaction which takes place when iron is placed in copper sulphate solution.
    **ii)** What kind of reaction is this?

# Answers to the 13+ Question bank

**1 a)** beaker  **b)** measuring cylinder  **c)** tripod

**2**

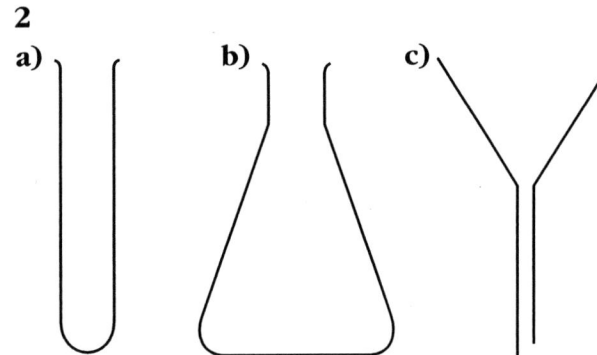

**3**

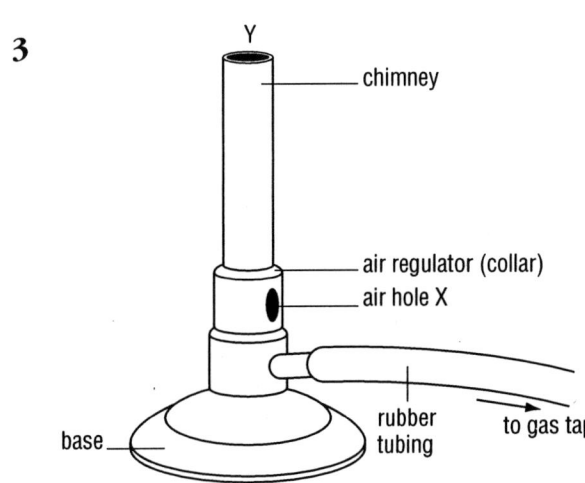

**4 a)** boiling  **b)** melting  **c)** condensing  **d)** freezing

**5 a)** B  **b)** A

**6 a)** magnesium and oxygen
  **b)** iron and sulphur

**7** The sand and salt are mixed with water and the salt dissolves in the water to make a salt solution but the sand does not dissolve. The sand and the salt solution are separated by filtration. The water escapes from the salt solution by evaporation and leaves salt crystals behind.

**8 a)** decomposition
  **b)** copper oxide and carbon dioxide
  **c)** solid (copper oxide) and gas (carbon dioxide)

**9** acid and base (alkali)

**10 a) i)** B  **ii)** A  **iii)** C
  **b) i)** C  **ii)** B  **iii)** A

**11 a)** water  **b)** carbon dioxide  **c)** oxygen  **d)** hydrogen

**12** $0.8 \text{ g/cm}^3$

**13 a)** oxygen and iron  **b)** iron oxide
  **c)** any method which keeps oxygen and water away from the surface of the iron, e.g. painting or covering in oil

**14 a)** calcium, carbon and oxygen
  **b) i)** decomposes to calcium oxide and carbon dioxide  **ii)** forms calcium chloride, water and carbon dioxide

**15 a)** metal  **b)** non-metal  **c)** metal  **d)** non-metal

**16 a)** magnesium, iron, copper, gold
  **b) i)** gold  **ii)** because it does not react with other elements easily
  **c) i)** magnesium  **ii)** hydrogen
  **d) i)** iron + copper sulphate
      → iron sulphate + copper
    **ii)** a displacement reaction

# Key Stage 3 test

**1** The chart is taken from a bottle of *Johnson's pH 5.5 Facial Wash*.

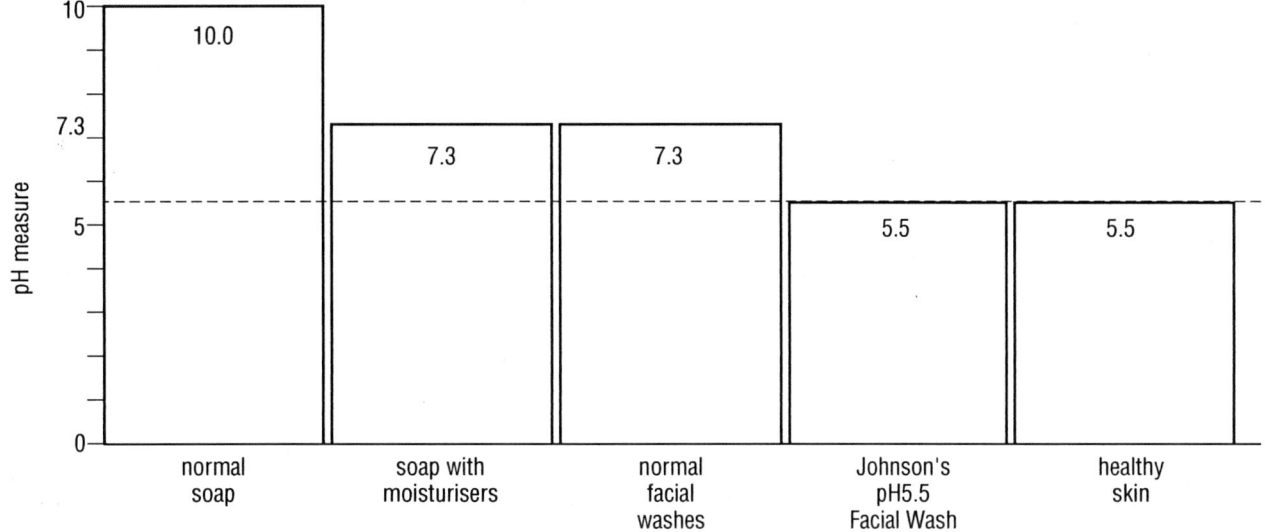

**a)** From the information in the chart give:
   **i)** a substance which is almost neutral, (1)
   **ii)** the substance which is most alkaline. (1)
**b)** Tick **one** box to describe Johnson's facial wash. (1)

   It is very alkaline.  ☐

   It is slightly alkaline.  ☐

   It is neutral.  ☐

   It is slightly acidic.  ☐

**c)** A bee sting is acidic. Which **one** of the substances given in the chart would be best to neutralise the sting? (1)

*(maximum 4 marks)*
[KS3/97/Sc/Tier 5–7/P1]

**2** A scientist investigates the paints used in oil paintings. She takes tiny pieces of yellow, blue and green paint and tries to dissolve them in different solvents. Her results are shown in the table.

| Solvent | Yellow paint | Blue paint | Green paint |
|---|---|---|---|
| water | yellow pieces are left | blue pieces are left | green pieces are left |
| ethanol | yellow pieces are left | clear blue liquid | clear blue liquid but yellow pieces are left |
| propanone | clear yellow liquid | clear blue liquid | clear green liquid |

**a)** Which solvent does **not** dissolve the blue paint? (1)

*(continued)*

She then uses chromatography to investigate the paints.

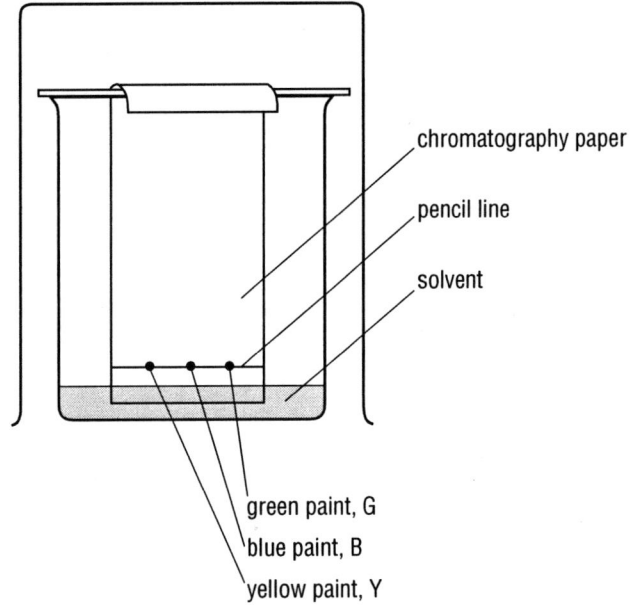

**b)** Only **one** of the solvents in the table will make all three paints move up the chromatography paper. Which solvent is this? (1)

**c)** The scientist then investigates the paint used in three different oil paintings. She takes tiny pieces of yellow, blue and green paint from each picture and uses chromatography to compare them. Her results are shown below.

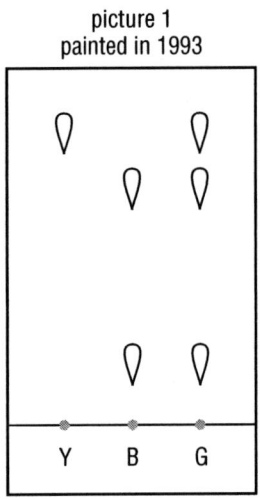
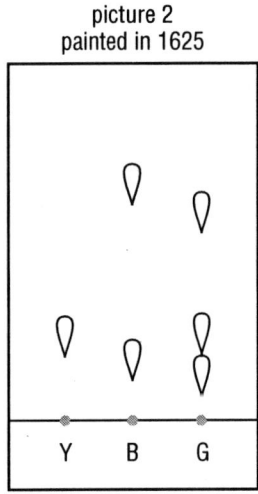
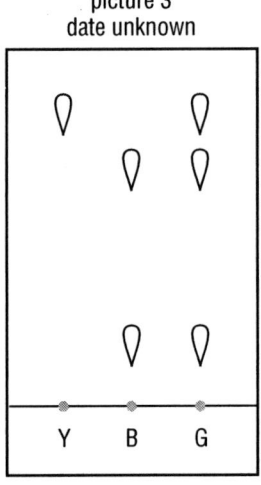

Which of the paints in the 1993 picture contains only **one** substance? Tick the correct box. (1)

yellow, Y ☐   blue, B ☐   green, G ☐

The scientist decides that picture 3 is probably recent and not from around 1625.

**d)** Look at the chromatography results for the three pictures. Explain how the scientist was able to decide this. (2)

*(maximum 5 marks)*
[KS3/97/Sc/Tier 5–7/P1]

**KEY STAGE 3 TEST**

**3** This question is about four chemical elements.
   **a)** The melting points and boiling points of the four elements are shown in the table. Complete the table to give the physical state (**solid**, **liquid** or **gas**) of each element at room temperature, 21°C.   (4)

| Element | Melting point in °C | Boiling point in °C | Physical state at room temperature, 21°C |
|---|---|---|---|
| bromine | 27 | 59 | |
| chlorine | 2 101 | 2 34 | |
| fluorine | 2 220 | 2 188 | |
| iodine | 114 | 184 | |

   **b)** Bromine can be solid, a liquid or a gas depending on the temperature. In which physical state will 10 g of bromine store the most thermal energy?   (1)
   **c)** Is bromine a **solid**, a **liquid** or a **gas** when the arrangement of particles is:
   **i)** far apart and random,   (1)
   **ii)** close together but random,   (1)
   **iii)** close together in a regular pattern?   (1)

   *(maximum 8 marks)*
   [KS3/97/Sc/Tier 5–7/P1]

**4** The exhaust gases of a car with a petrol engine are analysed during its 'MOT test'. The results are shown below.

| Gas | % volume |
|---|---|
| carbon monoxide | 3.0 |
| carbon dioxide | 13.0 |
| oxygen | 0.4 |
| other gases | 83.6 |

   **a)** The air going into the engine contains about 20% of oxygen. Explain why there is only 0.4% of oxygen in the exhaust gases coming out of the car engine.   (1)
   **b) i)** Petrol is a mixture of compounds which contains only carbon and hydrogen. Complete combustion of petrol produces carbon dioxide and **one** other substance. What is this other substance?   (1)
   **ii)** When petrol is burned in the car engine, carbon monoxide is produced as well as carbon dioxide. Explain why carbon monoxide is dangerous and may kill you.   (1)

   *(maximum 3 marks)*
   [KS3/97/Sc/Tier 5–7/P1]

**5** Aluminium and tin-plated steel are used to make cans for food and soft drinks. The table below shows the pH values of some soft drinks and cooked foods.

| Drinks and foods | pH value |
|---|---|
| cola | 2.0 |
| lemonade | 3.0 |
| rhubarb | 3.0 |
| beef | 7.0 |

*(continued)*

# KEY STAGE 3 TEST

**a)** Cans were first used about 150 years ago to store food for soldiers. The cans were made from unplated steel. The soldiers found that beef kept in steel cans was still good to eat after many months. However, they found that steel cans of rhubarb bulged, and when the cans of rhubarb were opened a gas escaped.
  **i)** Why were the steel cans **not** suitable for storing rhubarb? (1)
  **ii)** Name the gas that formed in the cans of rhubarb. (1)

Part of the reactivity series is given here:
magnesium
aluminium
zinc
iron (steel)
tin
copper
silver

**b)** In modern 'tin cans' the steel is covered with a thin layer of tin.
  **i)** Use the reactivity series to explain why 'tin cans' are better than steel cans for storing food. (1)
  **ii)** When 'tin cans' are dented, the layer of tin often cracks. What reaction might happen when the layer of tin is cracked? (1)
**c)** Many drink cans are now made of aluminium. Given the information in the reactivity series, why is this surprising? (1)

*(maximum 5 marks)*
[KS3/97/Sc/Tier 5–7/P1]

**6** The diagram shows part of a rock face. The igneous rock was formed when magma intruded into the sedimentary rock. The metamorphic rock was formed from the sedimentary rock as a result of the magma cooling.

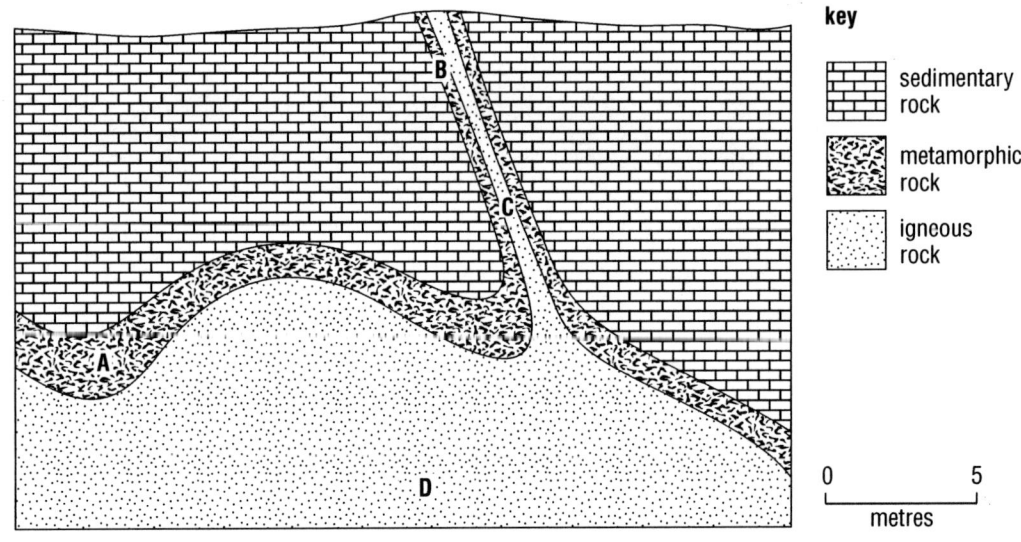

**a)** What is the change of state when magma crystallises to form igneous rock? (1)

From _____ to _____

**b)** The magma cooled more quickly at point C than at point D. What effect did this have on the size of the crystals formed at point C compared to the crystals at point D? (1)

**c)** Explain why a thicker band of metamorphic rock has formed at point A than at point B. (1)

*(maximum 3 marks)*
[KS3/97/Sc/Tier 5–7P1]

**7** The flow chart shows how zinc sulphate can be obtained.

$$\boxed{\text{zinc ore}} \rightarrow \boxed{\text{zinc oxide}} \rightarrow \boxed{\text{zinc}} \rightarrow \boxed{\text{zinc sulphate}}$$

**a)** In the reaction

zinc oxide → zinc

an element is removed from zinc oxide to leave zinc. Give the name of the element. (1)

**b) i)** Zinc sulphate can be made in a reaction between zinc and an acid. Give the name of the acid. (1)
**ii)** In the reaction between zinc and the acid, hydrogen is formed. Describe the test for hydrogen and the result if hydrogen is present. (1)
**iii)** How can crystals of zinc sulphate be formed from a dilute solution of zinc sulphate? (1)

*(maximum 4 marks)*
[KS3/97/Sc/Tier 5–7/P2]

**8** Five different rocks, A, B, C, D and E, are described in the table.
**a)** From the information given, classify each rock as igneous, metamorphic or sedimentary. One has been done for you. (4)

| Rock | Description of the rock's surface | Classification |
|---|---|---|
| A | The rock is crystalline. It has interlocking crystals of different colours and no layers can be seen. | |
| B | The rock is made of many rounded sand grains. | |
| C | The rock is crystalline with distinct black and grey bands. | metamorphic |
| D | Pieces of shells can be seen in the rock. | |
| E | The rock is very fine-grained, hard, and splits into thin layers. | |

**b)** Look at the descriptions of the rocks A, B, C, D and E.
**i)** Sheets of slate are used for roofing material. Which rock could be slate? (1)
**ii)** When limestone is weathered, fossils sometimes appear in the surface. Which rock could be limestone? (1)
**iii)** Granite is a crystalline rock. Its surface is speckled with a number of colours. It can be used for road chippings. Which rock could be granite? (1)

*(maximum 7 marks)*
[KS3/97/Sc/Tier 5–7/P2]

**KEY STAGE 3 TEST**

9 The diagrams show two Bunsen burners. One burner has the air hole closed, and the other has the air hole open.

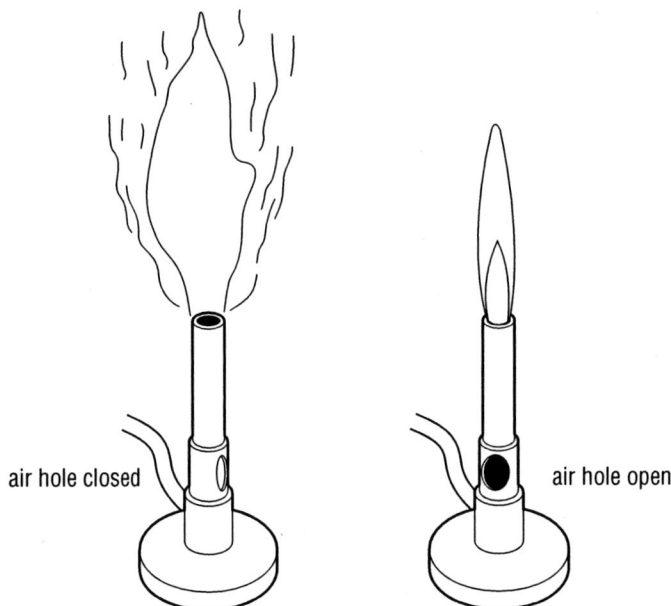

air hole closed   air hole open

    **a)** Explain why opening the air hole of a Bunsen burner makes the flame hotter. (1)
    **b)** Natural gas is methane, $CH_4$. It is burned in a Bunsen burner. Complete the word equation for the chemical reaction in the clear blue flame. (2)

    methane 1 _____ → _____ 1 _____

*(maximum 3 marks)*
[KS3/97/Sc/Tier 5–7/P2]

10 The table shows the chemical formulae of six minerals which occur naturally.

| Name of mineral | Chemical formula |
|---|---|
| saltpetre | $KNO_3$ |
| calcite | $CaCO_3$ |
| gold | Au |
| graphite | C |
| barytes | $BaSO_4$ |
| corundum | $Al_2O_3$ |

From the table give the name of **one** mineral which is:
**a)** a non-metallic element, (1)
**b)** a carbonate, (1)
**c)** a compound containing potassium, (1)
**d)** an electrical conductor at room temperature. (1)

*(maximum 4 marks)*
[KS3/97/Sc/Tier 5–7/P2]

KEY STAGE 3 TEST

**11** Air is a gas at room temperature. The chemical formulae below show some of the substances in the air.

$$Ar \quad CO_2 \quad H_2O \quad N_2 \quad Ne \quad O_2$$

**a)** Put these formulae in the correct columns in Table A to show which substances are elements and which are compounds. (1)

**Table A**

| Element | Compound |
|---|---|
|  |  |

**b)** Put the formulae in the correct columns in Table B to show whether the formula of each substance represents an atom or a molecule. (1)

**Table B**

| Atom | Molecule |
|---|---|
|  |  |

**c)** The coldest possible temperature is 'absolute zero', which is 2 273°C. As air is cooled towards absolute zero it liquefies. Table C gives the boiling points of the substances in the air.

**Table C**

| Formula | Boiling point in °C |
|---|---|
| Ar | 2 186 |
| $CO_2$ | 2 78 |
| $H_2O$ | 100 |
| $N_2$ | 2 196 |
| Ne | 2 246 |
| $O_2$ | 2 183 |

A sample of air at a temperature close to absolute zero is allowed to warm up. Which substance boils first? (1)

**d)** Each particle of neon can be represented by a circle. Carefully complete the diagrams below to show the arrangement of particles in neon gas and liquid neon. Use circles about ◯ in size. (4)

neon gas, Ne

liquid gas, Ne

*(maximum 7 marks)*
[KS3/97/Sc/Tier 5–7/P2]

**12** The diagram shows a geological section of a rock sequence. The letters show sites where rocks are found.

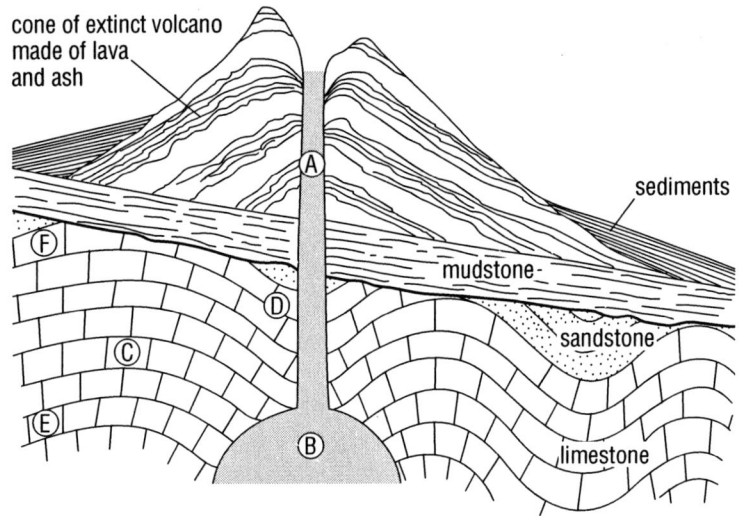

**a)** Some of the events which caused this rock sequence are listed below in alphabetical order.

1. Limestone deposited.
2. Mudstone deposited.
3. Rocks folded and eroded.
4. Sandstone deposited.
5. Volcano eroded to form sediment.
6. Volcano formed.

Suggest the order in which the events took place. Write the appropriate number in each box, starting on the left with the earliest. (1)

**b)** The photographs show thin sections of two igneous rocks. They are of equal magnification. One rock is from site A, and the other is from site B.

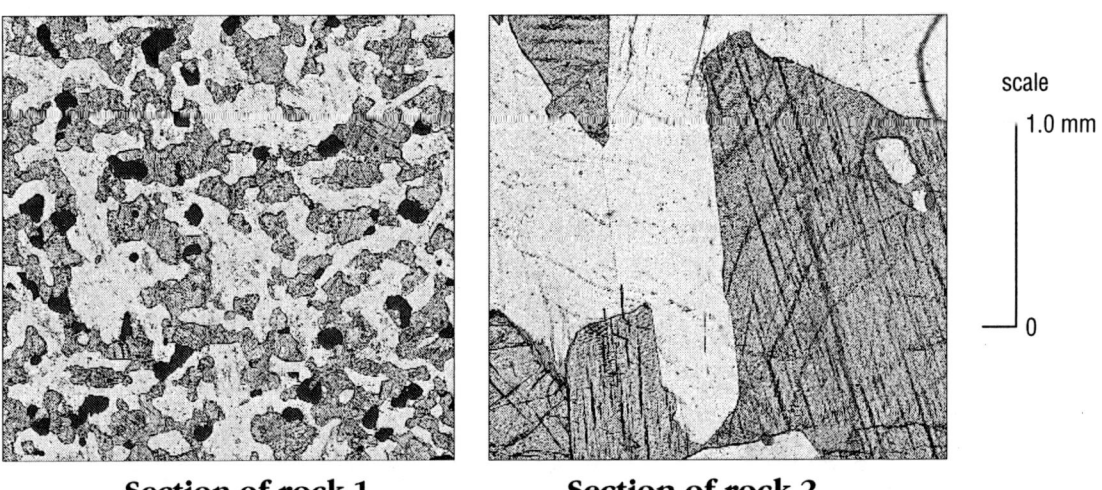

**Section of rock 1**    **Section of rock 2**

(Obtained from photographs in the *Atlas of igneous rocks and their textures*, by Mackenzie Donaldson and Guilford; sixth impression 1995; published by Addison Wesley Longman)

How do you know that rock 1 is more likely to be found at site A than at site B? (1)

*(continued)*

c) Limestone is mainly calcium carbonate. When limestone is heated strongly it forms calcium oxide and carbon dioxide.
   i) Write a balanced equation for this reaction. (1)
   ii) Sand grains may be found in limestone. Sand is mainly silica, $SiO_2$. A new mineral can be formed by the reaction of calcium carbonate with silica. This is calcium silicate, $CaSiO_3$. Write a balanced equation for this reaction. (1)
   iii) A different rock is formed when new minerals such as calcium silicate form within limestone. To which group of rocks does this new rock belong? (1)
   iv) From which site, C, D, E or F, would a specimen of limestone containing calcium silicate crystals be obtained? (1)

*(maximum 6 marks)*
[KS3/97/Sc/Level 8 and EP/Ext]

**13** The elements in group VII of the periodic table are known as the halogens.

|  | Melting point in °C | Boiling point in °C | Relative atomic mass | Colour of element at room temperature, 20°C |
|---|---|---|---|---|
| fluorine | 2 220 | 2 188 | 19 | very pale yellow |
| chlorine | 2 101 | 2 34 | 35.5 | greenish yellow |
| bromine | 2 7 | 59 | 80 | reddish brown |
| iodine | 114 | 184 | 127 | dark grey |
| astatine |  |  | 210 |  |

**a)** **i)** Predict the physical state of astatine at room temperature. (1)
   **ii)** Predict the colour of astatine at room temperature. Tick the correct box. (1)

   colourless ☐   yellow ☐   brown ☐   black ☐

**b)** The reactions of chlorine and bromine with some sodium salts are given below.

| Salt | Colour of salt solution | Colour after the addition of chlorine solution, which is greenish yellow | Colour after the addition of bromine solution, which is orange |
|---|---|---|---|
| sodium chloride | colourless | pale greenish yellow | orange |
| sodium bromide | colourless | orange | orange |
| sodium iodide | colourless | dark brown | dark brown |

   **i)** Use these observations to put the elements bromine, chlorine and iodine in order of reactivity, least reactive first. (1)
   **ii)** A solution of iodine, which is dark brown, is added to a solution of sodium bromide. What will be the colour of the resulting solution? (1)
**c)** Predict, with a reason, if there will be a reaction between:
   **i)** fluorine and sodium chloride solution, (1)
   **ii)** astatine and sodium iodide solution. (1)

*(maximum 6 marks)*
[KS3/97/Sc/Level 8 and EP/Ext]

**KEY STAGE 3 TEST**

**14** The apparatus shown below was set up. The 100 cm³ of clean, dry air was passed backwards and forwards across the hot copper powder. The volume of the air left in the syringe, when the apparatus had cooled back to room temperature, was 79 cm³.

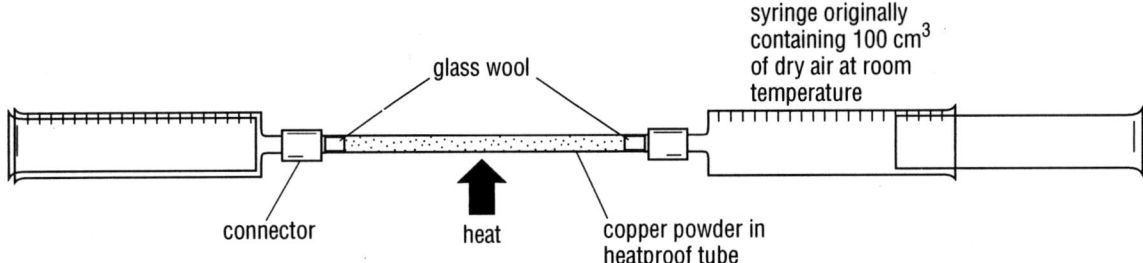

**a) i)** Why did the volume of air decrease? (1)
  **ii)** Why did the volume of air not decrease below 79 cm³? (1)
**b) i)** The surface of the copper was seen to be black at the end of the experiment. What is the chemical formula of the black solid which is formed? (1)
  **ii)** What type of reaction takes place in this experiment? (1)
  **iii)** Write a balanced equation for the formation of the black solid. (1)

*(maximum 5 marks)*
[KS3/97/Level 8 and EP/Ext]

**15 a)** The electronic arrangements of six elements are shown in the diagrams below. They are labelled A–F. Each electron is shown by a ×.

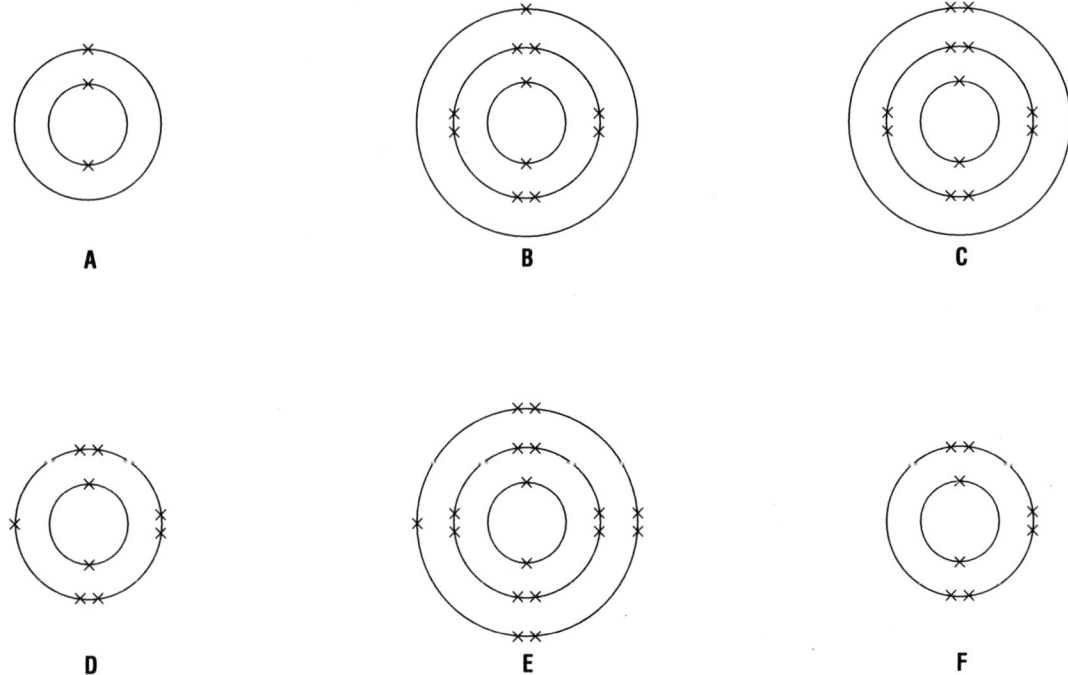

  **i)** Which element is in group VI of the periodic table? (1)
  **ii)** Three of the elements are metals. Give the letters of **two** elements which are metals. (1)
**b)** When element B reacts with another element, each atom of B loses its outer electron to leave an ion with a full outer shell of electrons. What will be the charge on the ion formed from an atom of element B? (1)

*(maximum 3 marks)*
[KS3/97/Level 8 and EP/Ext]

# Key Stage 3 test mark scheme

| Part | Mark | Answer | Additional guidance |
|---|---|---|---|
| 1 a) i) | 1 | any **one** from<br>• soap with moisturisers<br>• normal facial wash | *do **not** accept* 'soap' **or** 'pH 7.3' |
| ii) | 1 | • normal soap | *do **not** accept* 'soap' **or** 'pH 10.0' |
| b) | 1 | • It is slightly acidic. ✓ | if more than one box is ticked, award no mark |
| c) | 1 | • normal soap | *do **not** accept* 'soap' **or** 'pH 10.0' |
| Total | 4 | | |

| Part | Mark | Answer | Additional guidance |
|---|---|---|---|
| 2 a) | 1 | • water | |
| b) | 1 | • propanone | *do **not** accept* 'propane' **or** 'propone' |
| c) | 1 | • yellow ✓ | if more than one box is ticked, award no mark |
| d) | | **one mark is for identifying that the same paints were used in picture 3 and picture 1, and the other is for identifying the differences between the paints used in picture 3 and picture 2** | |
| | 1 | any **one** from<br>• the three paint colours are all the same in pictures 1 and 3<br>• the pattern of colours is the same in pictures 1 and 3<br>• the yellow and green paint are the same in pictures 1 and 3 | accept 'picture 1 matches picture 3' |
| | 1 | any **one** from<br>• the yellow **or** green paint in picture 3 is different from that in picture 2<br>• only the blue is the same in pictures 2 and 3<br>• only the blue paint is the same in the three pictures | |
| Total | 5 | | |

# KEY STAGE 3 TEST MARK SCHEME

| Part | Mark | Answer | Additional guidance |
|---|---|---|---|
| 3 a) | 1<br>1<br>1<br>1 | • bromine — liquid<br>• chlorine — gas<br>• fluorine — gas<br>• iodine — solid | |
| b) | 1 | • gas | |
| c) i)<br>ii)<br>iii) | 1<br>1<br>1 | • gas<br>• liquid<br>• solid | |
| Total | 8 | | |

| Part | Mark | Answer | Additional guidance |
|---|---|---|---|
| 4 a) | 1 | any **one** from<br>• used up in burning<br><br>• it reacted with fuel **or** petrol<br>• formed carbon dioxide **or** carbon monoxide | accept 'oxygen burned'<br>*do **not** accept* 'used up'<br><br>accept 'it has been turned into carbon dioxide' |
| b) i)<br><br>ii) | 1<br><br>1 | • water<br><br>• it is poisonous **or** toxic | accept 'steam' **or** 'hydrogen oxide'<br>*do **not** accept* 'hydroxide'<br>accept a reference to its being carried by the blood in preference to oxygen<br>accept 'it can form an explosive mixture with air'<br>*do **not** accept* 'it damages the lungs' **or** 'it is harmful' |
| Total | 3 | | |

# KEY STAGE 3 TEST MARK SCHEME

| Part | Mark | Answer | Additional guidance |
|---|---|---|---|
| 5 a) i) | 1 | • the acid **or** rhubarb reacted with the steel | accept 'the rhubarb reacts with it' <br> do **not** accept 'they bulged' **or** 'rhubarb is acid' **or** 'rhubarb has a low pH' |
| ii) | 1 | • hydrogen | accept '$H_2$' <br> do **not** accept 'H' |
| b) i) | 1 | any **one** from <br> • tin is less reactive than iron **or** steel <br> • tin is lower than steel | accept 'acid does not react with tin but does with steel' |
| ii) | 1 | **the answer may focus on either the inside or the outside of the can** <br> any **one** from <br> • the steel reacts with the food **or** is corroded by the acid in the food <br> • the iron **or** steel will rust **or** react with the air outside the can | |
| c) i) | 1 | • aluminium is more reactive than iron **or** steel **or** tin | accept 'aluminium is reactive **or** very reactive' <br> accept 'it's not surprising because the aluminium is covered with an oxide layer' <br> do **not** accept 'aluminium is high in the reactivity series' |
| Total | 5 | | |

| Part | Mark | Answer | Additional guidance |
|---|---|---|---|
| 6 a) | 1 | • from liquid to solid | **both** parts are required for the mark |
| b) | 1 | • they are smaller | |
| c) | 1 | any **one** from <br> • more energy has been transferred to it <br> • it is next to the larger volume of cooling magma **or** igneous rock | accept 'more heat was passed to it' <br> accept 'heat was passed to it from more magma' **or** 'it is closer to the main amount of magma' **or** 'only a small amount of magma got near to B' <br> do **not** accept 'it cooled more slowly' |
| Total | 3 | | |

Chemistry Now! 11–14 Teacher's Resource Book

# KEY STAGE 3 TEST MARK SCHEME

| Part | Mark | Answer | Additional guidance |
|---|---|---|---|
| 7 a) | 1 | • oxygen | *do **not** accept* 'oxide' |
| b) i) | 1 | • sulphuric acid | |
| ii) | 1 | • use a burning splint which lights the hydrogen **or** makes it go pop | accept 'it goes pop when lit' <br> *do **not** accept* 'use a glowing splint' |
| iii) | | **the mark is for concentrating the solution, or for a process which leads to crystallisation occurring** | |
| | 1 | any **one** from <br> • warm it **or** heat it gently <br> • leave it to stand <br> • let the water evaporate <br> • make it more concentrated | *do **not** accept* 'heat it' <br> accept 'leave by the window' <br><br> *do **not** accept* 'heat it until all the water has gone' **or** 'heat until dry' |
| Total | 4 | | |

| Part | Mark | Answer | Additional guidance |
|---|---|---|---|
| 8 a) | | | |
| | 1 | • A — igneous | |
| | 1 | • B — sedimentary | |
| | | • C | |
| | 1 | • D — sedimentary | |
| | 1 | • E — metamorphic | |
| b) i) | 1 | • E | |
| ii) | 1 | • D | |
| iii) | 1 | • A | |
| Total | 7 | | |

# KEY STAGE 3 TEST MARK SCHEME

| Part | Mark | Answer | Additional guidance |
|---|---|---|---|
| 9 a) | 1 | any **one** from<br><br>• more air **or** oxygen<br><br>• better mixing gives more combustion **or** more efficient burning | accept 'gas reaching the flame already has air **or** oxygen mixed in it'<br><br>accept 'better **or** faster combustion'<br><br>accept the converse, i.e. arguments applied to a Bunsen with a closed air-hole |
| b) | 1<br>1 | • oxygen<br>• carbon dioxide + water | do **not** accept 'air'<br>**both** products are required for the mark<br>products may be in either order<br>accept 'carbon monoxide + water'<br>disregard any reference to heat **or** energy<br>accept correct formulae for words<br>the equation need not be balanced |
| Total | 3 | | |

| Part | Mark | Answer | Additional guidance |
|---|---|---|---|
| 10 a) | 1 | • graphite | do **not** accept 'C' |
| b) | 1 | • calcite | do **not** accept '$CaCO_3$' |
| c) | 1 | • saltpetre | do **not** accept '$KNO_3$' |
| d) | 1 | • gold **or** graphite | do **not** accept 'Au' **or** 'C' |
| Total | 4 | | |

*Chemistry Now! 11–14 Teacher's Resource Book*

# KEY STAGE 3 TEST MARK SCHEME

| Part | Mark | Answer | Additional guidance |
|---|---|---|---|
| **11a)** | 1 | • <table><tr><th>Element</th><th>Compound</th></tr><tr><td>Ar<br>$N_2$<br>Ne<br>$O_2$</td><td>$CO_2$<br>$H_2O$</td></tr></table> | **all six** formulae are required for the mark |
| **b)** | 1 | • <table><tr><th>Atom</th><th>Molecule</th></tr><tr><td>Ar<br>Ne</td><td>$N_2$<br>$O_2$<br>$CO_2$<br>$H_2O$</td></tr></table> | **all six** formulae are required for the mark |
| **c)** | 1 | • Ne **or** neon | |
| **d)** | 1 | • up to ten randomly arranged particles spaced throughout the box<br>    accept just one particle<br>    do **not** accept an empty box | |
| | 1 | • most of the particles are not in contact with each other | |
| | 1 | • the box almost full of particles of neon, more than 50% of which are touching each other | |
| | 1 | • the particles are randomly arranged<br>    if the level of the liquid is drawn then accept the circles drawn correctly below the liquid level | |
| **Total** | 7 | | |

# KEY STAGE 3 TEST MARK SCHEME

| Part | Mark | Answer | Additional guidance |
|---|---|---|---|
| 12a) | 1 | • 1 4 3 2 6 5 | **all six** in the correct order are required for the mark |
| b) | 1 | • it has smaller crystals | accept 'it has smaller grains' |
| c) i) | 1 | • $CaCO_3 \rightarrow CaO + CO_2$ | *do **not** accept* a word equation |
| ii) | 1 | • $CaCO_3 + SiO_2 \rightarrow CaSiO_3 + CO_2$ | *do **not** accept* a word equation |
| iii) | 1 | • metamorphic | accept 'marble' |
| iv) | 1 | • D | |
| Total | 6 | | |

| Part | Mark | Answer | Additional guidance |
|---|---|---|---|
| 13a) i) | 1 | • solid | |
| ii) | 1 | • black ✓ | if more than one box is ticked, award no mark |
| b) i) | 1 | • iodine<br><br>bromine<br><br>chlorine | **all three** elements in the correct order are required for the mark<br><br>*do **not** accept* 'iodide, bromide, chloride' **or** 'sodium iodide, sodium bromide, sodium chloride' |
| ii) | 1 | • dark brown | accept 'brown' |
| c) i) | 1 | • yes, because fluorine is more reactive than chlorine | **both** the prediction and the reason are required for the mark<br><br>accept 'fluorine is above chlorine' **or** 'fluorine is very reactive' **or** 'chlorine is less reactive than fluorine' **or** 'chlorine is below fluorine'<br><br>accept 'fluorine reacts with water'<br><br>accept 'fluorine is higher in the periodic table than chlorine'<br><br>*do **not** accept* 'fluorine is more reactive than sodium chloride' **or** 'fluoride is more reactive than chloride' **or** 'because fluorine is stronger' |
| ii) | 1 | • no, because iodine is more reactive than astatine | **both** the prediction and the reason are required for the mark<br><br>accept 'iodine is above astatine' **or** 'astatine is less reactive than iodine' **or** 'astatine is below iodine' **or** 'astatine is very unreactive'<br><br>accept 'astatine is radioactive and does not last long enough to react'<br><br>accept 'iodine is higher in the periodic table than astatine'<br><br>*do **not** accept* 'astatine is less reactive than sodium iodide' |
| Total | 6 | | |

Chemistry Now! 11–14 Teacher's Resource Book

# KEY STAGE 3 TEST MARK SCHEME

| Part | Mark | Answer | Additional guidance |
|---|---|---|---|
| 14a) i) | 1 | • copper reacted with oxygen from the air | accept 'copper reacted with **or** combined with the air' <br><br> *do **not** accept* 'some air reacted' **or** 'some copper reacted' <br><br> *do **not** accept* 'because some had become copper oxide' <br><br> *do **not** accept* 'oxygen **or** air was used up' |
| ii) | 1 | any **one** from <br><br> • all the oxygen had reacted <br> • no more oxygen left to react <br> • only one gas reacted which was 21% of the air <br> • there were only 21 cm$^3$ of oxygen | <br><br><br> accept 'copper did not react with nitrogen' <br> accept 'only ⅕ of air is oxygen' <br> accept 'because copper does not react with other gases in the air' |
| b) i) | 1 | • CuO | |
| ii) | 1 | any **one** from <br><br> • oxidation <br> • redox <br> • reduction | <br><br> *do **not** accept* 'corrosion' |
| iii) | 1 | • 2Cu + O$_2$ → 2CuO | accept 'Cu + ½ O$_2$ = CuO' <br><br> *do **not** accept* 'Cu + O → CuO' **or** 'Cu + O$_2$ → CuO$_2$' |
| Total | 5 | | |

| Part | Mark | Answer | Additional guidance |
|---|---|---|---|
| 15a) i) | 1 | • F | |
| ii) | 1 | any **two** from <br><br> • A <br> • B <br> • C | **two** letters are required for the mark |
| b) | 1 | • one positive **or** +1 **or** 1+ | accept 'B$^+$' **or** '+' **or** 'positive' <br><br> *do **not** accept* '1' |
| Total | 3 | | |

# Meeting the demands of the National Curriculum or Common Entrance Examination at 13+

The page references are to *Chemistry Now! 11–14* Pupil's Book.

| Key Stage 3, AT 3: Materials and their properties | Page | Common Entrance at 13+ syllabus detail | Page |
|---|---|---|---|
| Pupils should be taught:<br>**1. Classifying materials**<br>**Solids, liquids and gases**<br>a) to recognise differences between solids, liquids and gases, in terms of properties, e.g. *density, compressibility, ease of flow, maintenance of shape and volume*; | 15–18 | measurement of the mass and volume and calculation of the density of regularly-shaped solids and of irregularly-shaped solids (using the displacement of water to find the volume) and of liquids will continue to be examined in the physics section of the Common Entrance examination. So too will the fact that air has mass and that it is possible to measure its density. | |
| b) a simple model of solids, liquids and gases, in terms of the arrangement and movement of particles; | 23–24 | a qualitative approach only is required. | 23–24 |
| c) how the particle theory of matter can be used to explain the properties of solids, liquids and gases, including changes of state, gas pressure and diffusion; | 24–27, 31 | knowledge of the meaning of the words *atom* and *molecule* and awareness of the particle model of matter. [A knowledge of ions and of diffusion will not be examined.] | 30, 51–52, 176 |
| **Elements**<br>d) that elements consist of atoms and that all atoms of the same element contain the same number of protons; | 47–54 | understanding of the term *element* as used in chemistry and the idea that samples of the same element contain the same type of atom. [An understanding of atomic structure in terms of protons etc. will not be examined.] | 47–52 |
| e) that elements can be represented by symbols and that the periodic table shows all the elements. | 54–56, 106, 167–175 | [Knowledge of chemical symbols and formulae and of the details contained in the periodic table will not be examined.] | |
| **Compounds**<br>f) how some elements combine through chemical reactions to form compounds, e.g. *water, carbon dioxide, magnesium oxide, sodium chloride*; | 33, 57, 64–65, 105 | understanding of the idea that elements combine to give compounds whose properties differ from those of the constituent elements. Burning of some elements in oxygen, e.g. carbon, sulphur, iron, magnesium. Reaction between pairs of elements, e.g. iron + sulphur, copper + sulphur, aluminium + iodine (in fume cupboard or outside) but not sodium in chlorine. | 33<br><br>107<br>64–65, 105 |
| g) that compounds have a definite composition and to represent compounds by formulae. | 33, 176–178 | [Representation by formulae is not required.] | |
| **Mixtures**<br>h) that mixtures, e.g. *air, sea water*, contain constituents that are not combined; | 33–35, 77 | knowledge that air is a mixture of gases and the approximate percentages of nitrogen, oxygen and the relatively small proportion of other gases in its composition. Uses of oxygen. Carbon dioxide as a product of respiration and a raw material for photosynthesis. | 77<br><br><br>80<br>58 |

# MEETING CURRICULUM DEMANDS

| Key Stage 3, AT 3: Materials and their properties | Page | Common Entrance at 13+ syllabus detail | Page |
|---|---|---|---|
| i) about methods, including filtration, distillation and chromatography, that can be used to separate mixtures into their constituents; | 37–46 | knowledge of the following:<br>• evaporation to recover a solute and the testing of water purity by measurement of its boiling point;<br>• simple distillation to recover a solvent from a solution and fractional distillation to recover ethanol (alcohol) from wine or beer; use of the Liebig condenser;<br>• paper chromatography to separate a mixture of two or more coloured solutes from a solution;<br>• filtration to remove insoluble solids from a suspension.<br>[Distillation of crude oil is not required.] | 41, 32<br><br>43–45<br><br>42<br><br>39–40 |
| **Metals and non-metals**<br>j) that most metallic elements are shiny solids at room temperature, that most are good thermal and electrical conductors and that a few are magnetic; | 104 | understanding of the terms *conductor* and *insulator* in both electrical and thermal contexts. Simple physical properties of materials and reasons for their use in everyday situations. Reference to the substitution of plastics for metals for certain uses. | 104<br>120–137<br>132–133 |
| k) that most non-metallic elements vary widely in their physical properties, that many are gases at room temperature and that most are poor thermal and electrical conductors;<br><br>l) to use these properties to classify elements as metals or non-metals; | 104<br><br><br><br>104–106 | appreciation of the grouping of elements into metals and non-metals according to physical characteristics such as electrical conductivity, shininess, malleability and according to whether they give acidic or basic oxides. (Carbon, copper, iron, magnesium, sulphur and zinc are suitable examples for experiments on burning the elements in air and testing the oxides. Calcium and sodium, if included, must be handled only by the teacher.) | 104<br><br>105–106 |
| **2. Changing materials**<br>**Physical changes**<br>a) that when physical changes, e.g. *changes of state*, *formation of solutions*, take place, mass is conserved; | 22 | understanding of the terms *solution*, *solvent*, *solute*, *insoluble* and *dissolving*. Knowledge that when soluble solids disappear in solution a chemical change is not involved and that a solution is a mixture which may be separated using physical techniques. | 35–36 |
| b) that solutes have different solubilities in different solvents and at different temperatures; | 36–37 | the abundance of water in nature, including its existence as vapour in the air, the water cycle (see KS2); use of anhydrous copper sulphate and anhydrous cobalt chloride to test for the presence of water vapour in the air. The domestic water supply; need for filtration; differences between sea, tap and distilled water (demonstrated by evaporation); importance of water as a solvent. Knowledge of ethanol and propane as alternative solvents to water but exclude chlorinated hydrocarbons. | 22–23<br><br>62<br>41<br><br><br>37<br>37 |
| c) that different materials change state at different temperatures; | 31–32 | understanding of the terms *melting*, *freezing*, *boiling*, *condensation*, *evaporation* and *sublimation*. | 24–26 |
| d) to relate changes of stage to energy transfers; | 24–26 | link this with **1b**). | |
| e) how materials expand and contract with changes in temperature and that the forces that result are sometimes considerable. | 24, 29, 100 | [See AT4: Physical processes.] | |

# MEETING CURRICULUM DEMANDS

| Key Stage 3, AT 3: Materials and their properties | Page | Common Entrance at 13+ syllabus detail | Page |
|---|---|---|---|
| **Geographical changes** | | | |
| f) how rocks are weathered by expansion and contraction and by the freezing of water. | 99–101 | [Not examined] | |
| g) that the rock cycle involves sedimentary, metamorphic and igneous processes that take place over different timescales. | 101–103 | [Not examined] | |
| h) that rocks are classified as sedimentary, metamorphic or igneous on the basis of their processes of formation and that these processes affect their texture and the minerals they contain. | 95–99 | [Not examined] | |
| **Chemical reactions** | | | |
| i) that when chemical reactions take place, mass is conserved. | 51–52, 177 | [Not examined] | |
| j) that virtually all materials, including those in living systems, are made through chemical reactions; | 57–58, throughout | many examples of such reactions are given in other sections. | throughout |
| k) to represent chemical reactions by word equations; | 57, 61–66 | construction of word equations for simple chemical reactions. | 57, 61–66 |
| l) that there are different types of reaction, including oxidation and thermal decomposition; | 58–66 | heating substances: | |
| | | • copper and magnesium to illustrate combustion and oxidation. Also the combustion of methane and similar fuels; | 64–65 |
| | | • hydrated copper(II) sulphate, hydrated cobalt chloride, copper carbonate and potassium manganate(VII) to illustrate thermal decomposition; | 61–62 |
| | | • copper oxide, zinc oxide and magnesium oxide (previously dried in an oven) to illustrate that some substances do not change chemically when heated; | 62 |
| | | • the action of heat on a mixture of carbon and copper oxide to illustrate reduction and oxidation. | 65 |
| | | Understanding that when things burn in air they are reacting with the oxygen. Experience of the glowing splint test for oxygen and the lime water test for carbon dioxide. Identification of the products of combustion, e.g. of a candle. Importance of oxygen as a reactant in respiration. | 82–84<br><br><br><br>80 |
| m) that useful products can be made from chemical reactions, including the production of metals from metal oxides; | 120–132, 139–147 | awareness that chemical reactions are needed for the extraction of copper, iron and aluminium from their ores. Recognition of chemical change by the new substances that are formed. | 123–132 |
| n) about chemical reactions, e.g. *corrosion of iron, spoiling of food*, that are generally not useful; | 89–90 | rusting as an example of corrosion. Food oxidation is essentially the process of respiration. [Spoiling of food will not be examined.] | 89–90 |
| o) that energy transfers that accompany chemical reactions, including the burning of fuels, can be controlled and used; | 82–86 | how to use the Bunsen burner for gentle warming, vigorous heating etc. Effect of air supply on the flame; relative temperatures of different parts of the roaring flame. | 84–85 |
| p) about possible effects of burning fossil fuels on the environment; | 153–157 | knowledge that air is often polluted by sulphur dioxide and carbon monoxide and the sources of these pollutants. The effect of burning fossil fuels. [Production and effects of ozone and oxides of nitrogen are not required.] | 153–157 |

## MEETING CURRICULUM DEMANDS

| Key Stage 3, AT 3: Materials and their properties | Page | Common Entrance at 13+ syllabus detail | Page |
|---|---|---|---|
| **3. Patterns of behaviour** | | | |
| **Metals** | | | |
| a) the reactions of metals with oxygen, water and acid; | 107–109 | copper, iron, magnesium and zinc are suitable examples for experiments. This list could be extended to aluminium and lead for work with dilute acids. If included, calcium and sodium must be handled only by the teacher. Experience of the lighted splint test for hydrogen. | 107–109<br><br><br><br>108 |
| b) the displacement reactions that take place between metals and solutions of salts of other metals; | 109–110 | displacement reactions between metals and solutions of the sulphates of other metals. | 109–110 |
| c) how a reactivity series of metals can be determined by considering these reactions; | 110–111 | candidates should be able to use the reactivity series of metals to deduce that those higher in the series might burn more vigorously in air, react faster with water and dilute acids and replace a lower metal from its oxide. The uses of metals low down the series, such as lead and copper, for roofing and piping; the need for methods of covering the surface when the more reactive iron is used; the exceptional lack of reactivity of the precious metals, silver and gold, which makes them useful for jewellery and electrical contacts. Reference should be made to the fact that most metals are not found in their free state and that chemical reactions are necessary to extract metals from their ores. | 110<br><br><br>108<br><br>90<br><br>121–123<br><br><br>120 |
| d) how this reactivity series can be used to make predictions about other reactions; | 110 | | |
| **Acids and bases** | | | |
| e) that pH is a measure of the acidity of a solution; | 73–74 | awareness of the use of the pH scale; the reaction between acids and alkalis (or bases). | 73–74 |
| f) to use indicators to classify solutions as acidic, neutral or alkaline; | 72–73 | experience of testing substances with different indicators, including full range or universal indicator. Understanding that substances can be acidic, alkaline or neutral. | 72–73 |
| g) the reactions of acids with metals and bases, including carbonates, to form salts; | 70–72, 65 | neutralisation and salt formation. The addition of sodium hydroxide solution to dilute hydrochloric acid to illustrate neutralisation and salt formation on evaporation of the neutral solution. Alternatively, salt formation could be illustrated by adding copper oxide or copper carbonate to warm dilute sulphuric acid and evaporating gently. [Titration will not be required.] | 65, 74 |
| h) some everyday applications of neutralisation, e.g. *the treatment of indigestion, the treatment of acid soil*; | 74–76 | medical and agricultural applications. | 74–76 |
| i) how acids in the atmosphere can lead to corrosion of metal and chemical weathering of rock; | 100–101, 155 | knowledge that carbon dioxide dissolves in water to form an acid and that rain is slightly acidic. A specific knowledge of limestone; its chemical composition, decomposition when heated, reaction with dilute hydrochloric acid; uses as a building material and for the production of agricultural lime. A specific knowledge of the weathering effect of acid rain on limestone. | 100–101<br><br>59<br><br><br><br>60<br>100 |